T0132184

WHAT THEY DON'T LEARN YOU IN SCHOOL

OR Essential Competencies for Lifelong Employability

C. D. JAMES

authorHOUSE®

AuthorHouse™
1663 Liberty Drive
Bloomington, IN 47403
www.authorhouse.com
Phone: 833-262-8899

Published by AuthorHouse 02/07/2024

ISBN: 979-8-8230-1919-4 (sc)
ISBN: 979-8-8230-1920-0 (hc)
ISBN: 979-8-8230-1918-7 (e)

Library of Congress Control Number: 2023923773

Print information available on the last page.

This book is printed on acid-free paper.

CONTENTS

ABOUT THE BOOK

"Knowledge is not power; it is potential. *Action is power.* And inspiration is the spark that puts knowledge into action. Inspiration comes from within, providing the energy and enthusiasm to achieve results."

—C. D. James

May you be inspired by this book to take actions that will increase the probability of successful long-term employability. This book is about transferring knowledge to you, knowledge that, as reported and confirmed by business leaders, "they" did not "learn" you in school. Identified shortcomings that are included in this book are foundational skills, tools, and competencies that are important to success in your life and your career.

We are in the midst of the fourth Industrial Revolution, characterized by technological innovations such as artificial intelligence, bots, drones, big data, virtual reality, blockchains, self-driving vehicles, etc. It has been predicted that these changes could impact up to 50 percent of existing jobs. Some of the competencies for what are labeled as "new collar" jobs include the following:

- teamwork/interdisciplinary collaboration
- diversity of perspectives
- understanding of artificial intelligence
- agility
- adaptability to software
- big data/data-driven decision-making and critical thinking
- competent lifelong learning with skills and credentials, ensuring lasting employability

The skills and competencies highlighted in this book are foundational, applicable to almost every career, and many are transferrable to your personal life. Here are suggestions on how best to use this book:

- There is an opportunity to learn and then an opportunity to apply. This application is the action portion of the above "knowledge is not power" quote. The shorter the time between these two events, the better. Recognize that we learn and retain by doing, not just reading a book or a chapter. Hence, I recommend referencing specific chapters in advance of the opportunity to apply the learning.

- It is essential that you understand the basic principles of each competency and apply them in real-time situations (e.g., the principle that building trust is key to being seen as an authentic leader).

- For some competencies, such as project management, I have included an overview as the topics are best covered, if necessary, in more comprehensive coursework. A fundamental understanding of PM principles will, however, prove helpful.

- In addition to implementing the principles, you may consider teaching them to others (e.g., lunch-and-learn sessions) since that is the second-best way to retain knowledge.

ABOUT THE AUTHOR

With a successful career spanning fifty-five years of diversified corporate and entrepreneurial experience, Charles James is imminently qualified to share his knowledge of the essential competencies for lifetime employability. He was CFO of a medical device start-up, recently sold, and is the former CEO of an Indianapolis-based software-as-a-service company. Charles has experience in manufacturing, health care, higher-ed, government, and software. He has held senior level executive positions in several large companies (General Motors) and small start-ups (TriMedx, AXS Imaging, eGov Strategies, Red Point Medical 3D, and Spigot Guard). Charles earned an undergraduate degree from Ohio State University and an MBA from the University of Dayton. He also attended Harvard University's program for management development. Charles spent time with Dr. W. Edwards Deming (quality), Phil Thomas (total cycle time), and Eli Goldratt (theory of constraints). He frequently provides advice/coaching to entrepreneurs and is involved in several start-ups. Charles was a member of the business school advisory board at Butler University for twelve years. At Butler, he also helped establish an MBA leadership coaching program, was a coach to MBA students, and served briefly as an adjunct professor. Charles has recruited, hired, fired, and mentored many in his long career. His passions include leadership, entrepreneurship, and improving the education system.

A LIFELONG LEARNING/EMPLOYABILITY MINDSET

"The illiterate of the twenty-first century are not those
who cannot read and write but those who cannot learn,
unlearn, and relearn."

—Alvin Toffler

By various accounts, the half-life of a skill is between three and five years,
meaning half of what we learn today will become obsolete in less than five
years. The fourth Industrial Revolution, as many call it, has ushered in
rapid, sweeping changes in what organizations do, how they do it, and for
many, even why they do it. To flourish in this new environment, each of us
must, as Toffler suggests, continually learn, unlearn, and relearn new skills
and competencies. We all must embrace lifelong learning, which ensures
lifelong employability.

The old model of competency and knowledge accumulation is best
illustrated in this T-shaped profile:

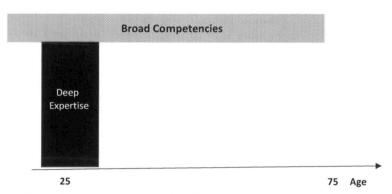

Source: N. van Dam, *Learn or Lose*, Breukelen, Netherlands, Nyenrode Publishing,
November 2016

As shown in this model, employees obtain deep expertise in one
discipline/competency early in their careers, supplemented over their
working lives with on-the-job development opportunities.

An M-shaped lifelong learning model reflects increases in life
expectancy and the accelerating half-life of knowledge:

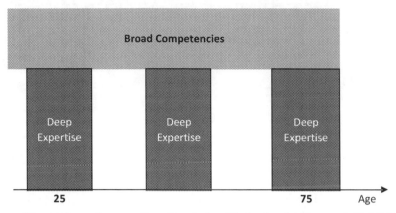

Source: N. van Dam, *Learn or Lose*, Breukelen, Netherlands, Nyenrode Publishing, November 2016

As this model implies, for employees to stay relevant, there is a need for deep expertise in several areas supplemented over their expected extended working lives with on-the-job development opportunities.

If, as some predict, artificial intelligence impacts up to half of all work activities, we must take seriously the need to remain relevant by continuously preparing for lifetime employability and engaging in lifetime learning. Reskilling and rewiring are about continually and successfully adapting as the economy evolves.

This book covers skills and competencies essential to ensuring employment relevance, now and in the future. Many of the competencies are not specifically taught in school or college, and employers have raised concerns about the lack of many of these competencies as they seek employees. I am confident that you have read about employer needs for many of the following competencies and/or tools:

- critical thinking
- communication
- effective presentations
- effective meetings
- familiarity with technology
- negotiating
- persuading others
- software tools
- listening

- brainstorming
- project management basics
- choosing the right metrics
- finance 101
- time management
- leadership/management
- etiquette

In addition to the soft skills and competencies detailed in this book, you should also consider the need for an understanding of the following hard skills that are growing in demand as the digital economy evolves. An understanding of these hard skills is typically obtained through coursework or specific training.

- cybersecurity and privacy
- data analytics / big data / data-driven decision-making
- artificial intelligence
- website design / coding
- cloud computing
- hyperconverged infrastructure
- blockchain knowledge
- data visualization
- cryptocurrency

Distinguish yourself professionally by developing a blend of competencies that cover the foundational soft skills identified in this book along with one or more of these new evolving competencies shown above, which may impact your organization. The goal is lifelong employability. The future will be about just-in-time, relevant education, not necessarily getting a degree. And as the saying goes, "If it is to be, it is up to me."

Right now, most of us are likely in a comfort zone, not realizing the importance of lifelong learning to our futures. By acquiring this book, you have taken the first step in moving out of your comfort zone to explore new skills, competencies, and/or gaining an understanding of what is needed to succeed in this rapidly evolving world. I suggest that you skip to Chapter 6, *Changing Your Behavior*, to review helpful tips on making successful progress on your journey.

1 CRITICAL THINKING / ROOT-CAUSE ANALYSIS

Critical thinking is a vital skill that enables individuals to analyze and evaluate information, make sound decisions, and solve complex problems. Root-cause analysis is a critical-thinking technique that seeks to identify the underlying causes of an issue or problem. This chapter explores the importance of critical thinking and root-cause analysis in personal and professional contexts.

Critical thinking is essential in today's world because it enables individuals to make better decisions, solve complex problems, and analyze information objectively. It helps individuals evaluate different perspectives and consider evidence before arriving at a conclusion. Critical thinking also allows individuals to recognize biases and assumptions that may influence their decision-making processes.

Moreover, critical thinking is necessary for effective communication and teamwork. In today's globalized world, people from diverse backgrounds work together, and critical thinking helps them understand different perspectives and collaborate more effectively. Critical thinking is also essential in decision-making, as it enables individuals to assess the pros and cons of different options to make informed choices.

Root-cause analysis is a critical-thinking/analytical technique used to identify the underlying causes of a problem or issue. It is a systematic approach that aims to find the root cause of a problem, rather than just addressing the symptoms. Root-cause analysis helps individuals identify the underlying factors that contribute to a problem and develop effective solutions to prevent its recurrence.

Root-cause analysis is essential in various fields, including health care, manufacturing, and engineering. In health care, root-cause analysis is used to investigate adverse events and identify ways to prevent them from happening again. In manufacturing, it helps improve the quality of products and increase efficiency by identifying and addressing production problems. In engineering, it identifies design flaws and improves the reliability and safety of products.

Moreover, root-cause analysis is also valuable in personal contexts, such as problem-solving and decision-making. By identifying the root cause of a problem, individuals can develop effective solutions that address the underlying factors and prevent its recurrence. Root-cause analysis also helps individuals make informed decisions by considering the underlying factors and evaluating different options objectively.

Root causes are typically (1) ones within management's control, (2) can reasonably be identified, and (3) have specific underlying causes.

The following is a process that everyone should have in his or her toolkit:

1. **Collect data**: This step involves identifying all data relevant to the event being analyzed.
2. **Prepare a causal factor chart**: Causal factor charting is a technique used in incident investigation and root-cause analysis to identify the underlying causes and contributing factors of an event or incident. It involves systematically analyzing the incident and its associated factors to identify the causal ones leading to the incident. The chart typically consists of a timeline of events leading up to the incident and includes categories such as equipment and human, organizational, and environmental factors. Each category is then broken down into more specific factors that contributed to the incident. The goal of causal factor charting is to identify the underlying factors that contributed to the incident and develop recommendations to prevent similar incidents from occurring in the future. Causal factor charting is often used in conjunction with other root-cause analysis, such as fishbone diagrams, fault-tree analysis, and event-tree analysis. Together, these techniques provide a comprehensive approach to incident investigation and help organizations improve safety and prevent future incidents.
3. **Root cause(s) identification**: This step involves preparation of a decision diagram, called a root-cause map, which is a tool used to visually display the underlying causes and contributing factors

of a problem or incident and enable informed decision-making by presenting information in a logical, structured way. It is a graphical representation of the causal relationships among the various factors that led to the problem, organized in a hierarchical structure that allows for clear understanding. The root-cause map typically consists of a series of boxes or bubbles, each representing a factor that contributed to the problem. The boxes are connected by arrows to show the causal relationships between them. The most significant, or root cause, is usually placed at the top of the map, with the factors that contributed to it branching off downward. Root-cause maps can be created in different formats, such as flowcharts, mind maps, or tree diagrams, depending on the complexity of the problem and the preference of the user. The map can also include additional information, such as data, evidence, and recommended actions to address each of the contributing factors. The purpose of a root-cause map is to provide a visual representation of the complex causal relationships among the various factors leading to the problem. By identifying the root causes, organizations can develop effective, corrective actions that address the underlying factors and prevent an issue's recurrence. Root cause-maps are commonly used in industries such as health care, manufacturing, and engineering but can be applied in any context where a problem needs to be solved and its root causes identified.

4. **Recommendations**: Following identification of the root causes, recommendations are developed for preventing a recurrence or improving a process.

The Five Whys Method of Root-Cause Analysis

The Five Whys method is a simpler version of the above-described root-cause analysis. It is helpful in peeling away symptoms of a problem to get to the root cause.

How it works: Individually or in a team setting ask why a situation is occurring. Look at the answer and ask the next *why*. You do this repeatedly until you have asked either five times or until you can no longer answer why. An example that took six *whys* follows:

Problem: On the way to work, your truck stops in the middle of the road.

1. *Why* did your truck stop?
   - It ran out of gas.

2. *Why* did it run out of gas?
   - Because I did not buy any on the way to work.

3. *Why* didn't you buy gas?
   - Because I did not have any money.

4. *Why* didn't you have any money?
   - Because I left my wallet in my other pants.

5. *Why* did you leave your wallet in your other pants?
   - Because I overslept and just quickly grabbed a pair of pants before darting out of the house.

6. *Why* did you oversleep?
   - I forgot to set my alarm for daylight saving time.

As you can see, this is a simpler approach to root-cause analysis and can be implemented very quickly.

PROJECT MANAGEMENT BASICS

This chapter is not intended to make you an expert in what can be a complicated and involved process. It is, however, intended to provide an overview of project management basics, including project definition, planning, execution, monitoring, and control. The chapter also discusses some common methodologies and software tools that can prove helpful.

Project management is essential because it helps ensure that projects are delivered on time and within budget while meeting the requirements of stakeholders. Effective project management can lead to increased efficiency, improved quality, and enhanced customer satisfaction while helping organizations to manage risks and minimize failures.

The following provides an overview of the key elements of project management, including project definition, planning, execution, monitoring, and control.

definition: The first step in project management is to define the project's scope, objectives, and deliverables. This involves identifying the project's stakeholders, understanding their needs and expectations, and defining goals and objectives. Project definition also involves identifying constraints, such as time, budget, and resources. The project manager must ensure that the project's objectives are realistic and achievable within the constraints of the project.

planning: Once the project's objectives have been defined, the next step is to develop a project plan. The project plan should include a detailed schedule, resource allocation, risk assessment, and budget. The project manager must ensure that the plan is comprehensive and covers all aspects of the project. The project plan should also be communicated to all stakeholders to ensure that everyone understands their roles and responsibilities.

execution: Project execution involves implementing the project plan. This includes managing the team, monitoring progress, and ensuring the project is on track to meet its objectives. The project manager must ensure that the project team has the necessary resources and support to execute the project plan. The project manager must also monitor progress and take corrective action when necessary to keep the project on track.

monitoring and control: Monitoring and control involves tracking the project's progress, identifying deviations from the plan, and taking corrective action to bring the project back on track. This involves monitoring milestones, tracking costs, and assessing risks. The project manager must also communicate the project's status to stakeholders and adjust the project plan, if necessary, to ensure that all objectives are met.

Several key methodologies are described below:

Agile project management is an iterative and flexible approach to management that focuses on delivering value to customers through collaboration, adaptability, and rapid feedback. Unlike traditional project management, which follows a linear, sequential approach, agile methodology emphasizes continuous improvement and adaptation, encouraging teams to work collaboratively and communicate regularly. Agile methodology prioritizes the delivery of working software in short cycles, or sprints, and encourages frequent inspections and adaptations to the project plan. This approach allows teams to respond quickly to changes in requirements, customer needs, or market trends, resulting in higher quality products delivered quickly and efficiently. Agile methodology has gained popularity in recent years, particularly in the software-development industry, where the fast pace of innovation and changing customer needs require a more adaptable approach.

Scrum is a framework used in project management based on the agile methodology. It is often used in software development projects but can be applied to any project that requires a collaborative team approach. The scrum framework consists of several roles, events, artifacts, and rules that help teams work together effectively to deliver valuable software, or other products. The main roles in scrum are the product owner, the scrum master, and the development team. The product owner is responsible for defining the product backlog, which is a prioritized list of features and requirements. The scrum master is responsible for ensuring the team follows the framework and removes any obstacles that may prevent them from achieving their goals. The development team is responsible for delivering a potentially releasable increment of the product at the end of each sprint.

The main events in scrum are the sprint, sprint planning, daily scrum, sprint review, and sprint retrospective. A sprint is a time period, typically two weeks, during which the team works to deliver a potentially releasable increment of the product. During sprint planning, the team decides what work they will do in the upcoming sprint. The daily scrum is a short daily meeting in which the team members discuss their progress and plan their work for the day. The sprint review is a meeting at the end of each sprint, where the team presents the work they have done to stakeholders and receives feedback. The sprint retrospective is a meeting where the team reflects on the previous sprint and identifies areas for improvement.

The main artifacts in scrum are the product backlog, the sprint backlog, and the increment. The product backlog is a prioritized list of features and requirements that the team works from. The sprint backlog is a subset of the product backlog, which the team commits to completing during the sprint. The increment is the sum of all the completed items in the product backlog.

Overall, scrum is a flexible framework emphasizing collaboration, communication, and continuous improvement. It can be used to manage projects of varying sizes and complexities and is particularly effective in projects with changing requirements or uncertain outcomes.

The critical path method (CPM) is a project management technique used often in the construction industry to identify the sequence of activities that must be completed on time to ensure a project is completed on schedule. CPM is particularly useful for complex projects with many interdependent activities, where delays in one activity can cause delays in subsequent ones and impact the overall timeline. The critical path is the longest sequence of activities that must be completed in order to finish the project on schedule. By identifying the critical path, project managers can focus on managing those activities and ensure they are completed on time. CPM involves creating a network diagram of all project activities and their dependencies, estimating the duration of each, and calculating the earliest and latest possible start and finish times. This allows project managers to identify which activities are critical and must be completed on time and which have some flexibility in their timing. The applicability of CPM extends beyond the construction industry and can be used in various fields including manufacturing, software development, and event planning.

The waterfall method is a traditional project management approach that follows a linear, sequential process, where each phase of a project must be completed before the next one can begin. The waterfall method is commonly used in software development, construction projects, and manufacturing, where project requirements are well-defined and the scope is unlikely to change. The phases of the waterfall method include requirements gathering, design, implementation, testing, and deployment. Each phase must be completed and signed off before the next phase can begin, making it easy to track progress and ensure that a project stays on track. This approach is suitable for projects with clearly defined objectives and well-understood requirements, where the outcome is predictable and the risks are low. However, the waterfall method has limitations in situations where requirements may change or evolve over time, as it is difficult to make changes once a phase has been completed. It is also less flexible than other approaches, making it unsuitable for projects that have a high degree of uncertainty or complexity.

Hybrid (aka structured agile) combines the best parts of agile and waterfall in a flexible yet structured approach. Hybrid follows the waterfall method of gathering and analyzing requirements initially. The balance is agile based, including emphasis on ongoing iterations related to implementation. Hybrid is best suited for medium-sized, moderately complex projects that have fixed budgets. While you have an idea of the end product, the methodology affords some flexibility.

Integrated Project Delivery (IPD) is a collaborative approach to project management that involves all stakeholders, including the owner, design team, and construction team, working together from the beginning of a project to achieve common goals. This methodology emphasizes early and ongoing collaboration among all team members, encouraging them to work together to develop solutions to any issues that may arise. The goal of IPD is to deliver high-quality projects on time and budget while maximizing value to all stakeholders. The IPD method promotes transparency and trust among all stakeholders, enabling them to work toward shared objectives and minimize risk. This approach is particularly suitable for complex projects where stakeholders may have different priorities or requirements. It is often used in the construction industry, where the complexity of building projects and the interdependence of project team members makes collaboration essential. However, the IPD method can be applied to any project where collaboration and teamwork are essential for success.

Projects Integrating Sustainable Methods (PRiSM) is a project management methodology designed to enable companies to manage projects while integrating environmental sustainability into their processes and thus reduce any negative ecological and social impact when completing a project. It is a structured, process-based approach that focuses on five areas of sustainable development (project objectives, resource efficiency, stakeholder engagement, environmental performance, life cycle assessment) and four key project phases (concerned groups, sustainability orientation, organizational orientation, results). It is useful for large projects where minimizing the environmental impact or reducing energy consumption is critical. It does require buy-in to sustainability principles by all involved parties and is best suited for large-scale real estate development projects or construction or infrastructure projects that can have adverse environmental effects.

Implementation

You are now armed with some basic knowledge of the various project management methodologies. Critical next steps include selection or recruitment of a project manager and the appropriate software to ensure a successful implementation.

Project Manager (PM)

Consider recruiting an experienced PM. During the interview process, explain your project and seek input on the best methodology to use and the appropriate software tools to implement it. Input will be informative as some candidates may suggest a more complex and involved process than you really need.

Project-Management Software

There are many software options, some more appropriate for the methodology being used and the complexity of the project. For example, I have had good experience with Jira in conjunction with agile-based software development. An experienced PM will be able to suggest appropriate software. Here are some popular project management software and the pros and cons of each:

1. **Trello**: Trello is a visual project management tool that uses boards, lists, and cards to help teams organize and prioritize their work. The tool is simple to use and has a free version for personal projects. Some pros of Trello are its user friendly interface, real-time updates, and integration with other tools, such as Slack and Google Drive. However, some cons of Trello include limited functionality for complex projects, a lack of advanced reporting, and limited customization options.

2. **Asana**: Asana allows teams to track their work, organize tasks, and collaborate in real time. Some pros of Asana include its flexible project management features, easy-to-use interface, and integration with other tools, such as Slack and Google Drive. However, some cons of Asana include a relatively steep learning curve for new users, limited customization options, and a higher cost compared to other project management tools.

3. **Monday.com**: Monday.com offers a visual and intuitive interface that can be customized to fit the needs of any team. Some pros of Monday.com include its flexibility, real-time updates, and integration with other tools, such as Slack and Google Drive. However, some cons of Monday.com include a higher cost compared to other project management tools, limited functionality for complex projects, and a lack of advanced reporting.

4. **Basecamp**: Basecamp focuses on collaboration and communication among team members. Some pros of Basecamp include its easy-to-use interface, real-time updates, and integration with other tools, such as Slack and Google Drive. However, some cons of Basecamp include limited functionality for complex projects, a lack of customization options, and a higher cost compared to other project management tools.

5. **Jira**: Jira is popular among software-development teams. It allows teams to track and manage tasks, bugs, and issues on a single platform. Some pros of Jira include its powerful project management features, extensive customization options, and integration with other tools, such as GitHub and Bitbucket.

However, some cons of Jira include a steep learning curve for new users, a complex interface, and a higher cost compared to other project management tools.

In summary, there are numerous software options available, and each has its own set of advantages and disadvantages. When choosing a project management tool, it is important to consider the needs of your team, the complexity of your projects, and your budget.

FINANCE 101

Everyone working should have some understanding of the financial aspects of running a business, even if you are not involved in making financial-related decisions. This is because financial performance is the backbone of any organization and directly impacts the long-term viability and sustainability of the company. When employees understand how the company generates revenue, manages expenses, and makes strategic investments, they are better equipped to make informed decisions and take actions that positively impact the bottom line. Furthermore, financial literacy among employees can lead to greater accountability and efficiency in the workplace, as employees are more aware of the financial implications of their actions and can contribute to the company's overall success. Ultimately, employees who understand the financial aspects of the company they work for could become better advocates for the business, driving growth and innovation and helping ensure the company's long-term success.

While in the world of accounting, each worker is considered an expense (I prefer to categorize them as an asset), it is essential that each of us understands where an organization is headed and how it is doing financially. Like all professions, the finance world has a jargon of its own. This chapter explains that jargon in simple terms and with examples, its relative importance, and how financial data is typically used. This will not make you a green-eyeshade-wearing, bean counter, but hopefully it will enable you to be a better-informed employee.

Accounting Principles and Definitions

To help ensure comparability among companies, the accountants of the world have developed some guidelines, or principles, called Generally Accepted Accounting Principles (GAAP), pronounced "gap." GAAP allows companies to record their results using an approach known as accrual accounting, which allows the bookkeepers to recognize revenue when a service or product is provided while also accruing/booking any expenses associated with that revenue, such as payroll or shipping. The accrual method is intended to provide a more accurate view of the profitability of the organization by matching expenses incurred, but not necessarily paid, with the revenue received or to be received from a sale. The *direct* expenses tied to revenue generated are called cost of goods sold. Operating expenses are considered the overhead of the business and generally consist of sales and general and administrative expenses, such as rent, utilities, insurance, administrative employees, etc. Another, simpler, non-GAAP approach is cash accounting, which as the name implies does not record anything as expense or revenue until cash is actually disbursed or received.

Understanding the Three Key Financial Statements

There are three interrelated statements that you should be aware of.

Income Statement aka Profit-and-Loss Statement

This statement indicates whether you are making money in the specific period shown, such as a month, quarter, or year. See the following example:

Income Statement for the Quarter
Ended September 30, 2023

Revenue	$	520,000
Cost of Goods Sold	$	(340,000)
Gross Profit	$	180,000
Less Operating Expenses	$	(95,000)
Depreciation Expense	$	(5,000)
Earnings before Interest and Taxes	$	80,000
Less Interest Expense	$	(15,000)
Earnings before Taxes	$	65,000
Taxes	$	(21,000)
Net Income	$	44,000

Note that an expense category named depreciation is shown. When you acquire a piece of equipment that will last over several years, you depreciate it in a consistent manner, such as on a straight-line basis (the above example is a $100,000 piece of equipment that is being depreciated over five years, or twenty quarters).

Balance Sheet or Statement of Financial Position

The statement of financial position, often referred to as the balance sheet, reflects the financial condition of an organization; hence, it is a critical statement, albeit just a snapshot of a certain point in time. The report summarizes the assets or resources, the obligations or what is owed, and the ownership on a specific day. An example follows:

Balance Sheet
(Also called "Statement of Financial Position")
As of September 30, 2023

Assets

Cash in Bank	$	65,000
Inventory	$	35,500
Accounts Receivable	$	28,000
Equipment / Fixed Assets	$	100,000
Less Accumulated Depreciation	$	(40,000)
Total Fixed Assets	$	60,000
Total Assets	$	188,500

Liabilities

Accounts Payable	$	24,000
Accrued Expenses: Payroll	$	20,000
Long-Term Debt	$	45,000
Total Liabilities	$	89,000

Owner's Equity

Stock	$	50,000
Retained Earnings	$	49,500
Total Owner's Equity	$	99,500
Total Liabilities and Owner's Equity	$	188,500

The categories are relatively self-explanatory. You will note that total assets equals total liabilities and owner's equity, hence the term balance sheet. Retained earnings represent what the company has earned (or in some cases lost) since it began business. Stock is an indication of the value the owners received when they put cash in the business to get it started. Liabilities are what is currently owed and assets reflect the investments in equipment, inventory, and cash, either in the bank or soon to be received from customers.

It is generally helpful to compare balance sheets from two periods to understand the progress of an organization (e.g., is it getting more liquid with higher cash and accounts receivable balances compared to amounts owed).

Cash Flow Statement

The cash flow statement shows what happened to the cash balance in an organization from one period to the next. It helps in understanding how well an organization is converting profits into cash and thus keeping it solvent. It may also show that the organization issued stock or borrowed money, potentially raising questions. Shown below is a simple cash flow statement:

Cash Flow Statement
For the Year Ended December 31, 2022

Cash Flow from Operations		
Net Income	$	410,000
Additions to Cash:		
Depreciation (a noncash write-off)	$	20,000
Decrease in Accounts Receivable	$	25,000
Increase in Accounts Payable	$	10,000
Subtractions from Cash:		
Increase in Inventory	$	(30,000)
Net Cash from Operations	$	435,000
Cash Flow from Investing		
Purchase of Equipment	$	(75,000)
Cash Flow from Financing		
Issuance of Stock	$	50,000
New Debt	$	100,000
Cash Flow for Year Ended Dec 2022	**$**	**510,000**
Memo: Cash Balance at Year End	$	745,000

As you can see from this simple example, the statement is useful in showing how changes in income and balance sheet accounts, such as accounts receivable, affect the cash balance. It also shows the impact on cash of capital spending for equipment purchases and debt or stock financing. It is an important analytical tool to assess the short-term viability of a company and understand how much cash is being generated from operations versus financing.

Financial Analyses

Thus far, you have been introduced to important accounting lingo plus the three key financial statements:

- The income statement, which shows how much profit or loss has been generated during a period.
- The balance sheet, which provides a snapshot of an organization's assets, liabilities, and owner's equity on a specific day.
- The cash flow statement, which tracks where cash came from and where it is being used.

Now, we will briefly review some of the financial ratios used to assess various aspects of an organization's financial results. These ratios are most useful when viewed in a trend format and/or compared to the ratios of other companies in the same industry.

Profitability

- **gross profit margin**: Gross profit (revenue less the cost of making a product) divided by revenue is a measure of relative profitability, before considering overhead or other expenses.
- **EBITDA margin**: This is EBITDA divided by revenue. EBITDA is earnings before interest, taxes, depreciation, and amortization
- **return on sales (ROS)**: Net income divided by revenue is a measure of how much is earned for every sales dollar.

- **return on assets**: Net income divided by total assets measures how efficiently an organization is using its assets to generate profits.
- **return on equity (ROE)**: Net income divided by owner's equity reflects how much an organization is generating as a percentage of the owner's investment.

Efficiency Ratios (Management of Assets and Liabilities)

- **asset turnover**: Revenue divided by total assets measures how good an organization is at employing its assets to generate revenue. The higher the number, the better.
- **days sales outstanding (DSO)**: The ending accounts receivable amount divided by average revenue per day (annual revenue divided by 365). This tells you how long on average it takes an organization to collect what it is owed. The lower the number, the better since this implies quicker collection of outstanding receivables from customers.
- **inventory days outstanding**: The average number of days inventory is held before it is sold. The longer it takes, the more cash is tied up. The calculation is average inventory / cost of sales times the number of days in the period (e.g., thirty). Average inventory is calculated by adding the beginning and ending inventory and then dividing the total by two. The cost of sales or cost of goods sold number comes from the income statement and represents the direct costs incurred in the production of goods or services.
- **days payable outstanding (DPO)**: Measures the average number of days an organization takes to pay its suppliers or effectively hold onto its cash. It is calculated by taking the ending accounts payable balance and dividing it by purchases per day (total cost of goods sold per year divided by 365 days).

Liquidity Ratios (Ability to Meet Current Financial Obligations)

- **current ratio**: Total current assets divided by total current liabilities is the prime measure of the ability of an organization to pay its bills. The higher the ratio, the greater the financial strength.
- **quick ratio**: Also known as the acid test, this ratio measures the ability to cover liabilities quickly without having to liquidate

inventory. It is current assets less inventory divided by current liabilities.

Leverage (Reliance on Debt)

- **debt to equity**: Total liabilities divided by owners' equity. This shows how much an organization has borrowed compared with how much the owners have invested. An organization is considered to be highly leveraged if this ratio is high, especially compared to others in the industry.
- **times interest earned or interest coverage**: This is EBITDA divided by interest expense and measures the margin of safety in making interest payments from operating profits.

Miscellaneous Financial Metrics

- **earnings per share (EPS)**: As the name implies, this is net income divided by the number of shares outstanding and is a widely watched performance indicator.
- **price earnings (PE)**: This is the current price of a share of stock in a publicly traded company divided by the previous twelve months' earnings per share. While this number varies by industry, the S&P 500 stock index has had an average ratio of 15.54, ranging from 5.31 in 1917 to 123.73 in May 2009.
- **employee productivity**: Sales per employee and net income per employee are two measures of operating efficiency, generally measured over time.
- **growth**: Year over year changes in revenues, net income, or EPS are measures that can highlight growth.

Analytical Tips

- It is helpful to look at trends versus point-in-time data, which may contain an anomaly.
- Compare similar-sized organizations, preferably in the same industry.
- Use numbers as a guide to improvement, not to judge people. And use them as the first step in root-cause analysis.

Need for a Balanced Scorecard

I would be remiss if I did not point out that running an organization is about more than just the financials. In their book *The Balanced Scorecard*, Drs. David Norton and Robert Kaplan identified the following balanced perspectives for measurement:

- financial—to succeed financially, how should we appear to our shareholders?
- customer—to achieve our vision, how should we appear to our customers?
- internal/business process—to satisfy our shareholders, what business processes must we excel at?
- learning and growth—to achieve our vision, how will we sustain our ability to change and improve.

The balanced scorecard emphasizes that financial and nonfinancial measures should be part of the information system for employees at all levels of the organization.

Admittedly, the finance world is rife with jargon. This chapter can be used as a reference guide of sorts as you work to understand the health of your organization.

CHOOSING THE RIGHT METRICS

"Tell me how you are going to measure and reward me, and I'll perform accordingly."

"No one is completely useless; you can always serve as a bad example."

—Widely recognized concepts not attributable to a specific author.

These two quotes are certainly relevant to one of the more critical responsibilities of a leader—choosing the right metrics, or what will be measured or monitored to track progress. Perverse behavior, misaligned goals, or an inappropriate sense of success are results of using the wrong metrics. Business metrics, also known as key performance indicators (KPIs), are measurable values used to track and analyze the performance of a business or organization. These metrics evaluate the success of a business in achieving its goals and objectives and identify areas for improvement.

Business metrics can be qualitative or quantitative and can be used to track a wide range of business activities, such as sales, revenue, customer satisfaction, employee productivity, website traffic, and social media engagement. Examples of commonly used business metrics include the following:

- revenue and profit margins
- customer acquisition and retention rates
- conversion rates
- return on investment (ROI)
- average order value (AOV)
- customer lifetime value (CLV)
- net promoter score (NPS)
- employee turnover rate
- time to market

Business metrics can be tracked in real time or over a specific period, such as daily, weekly, monthly, or quarterly. They are typically displayed in dashboards or reports and are used to make data-driven decisions to improve business performance.

Before considering the steps to choosing the right metrics, consider these "learning" examples:

- *Moneyball*, a bestseller by Michael Lewis, describes how the Oakland Athletics discovered that the metrics the team's scouts used to evaluate and select baseball players were totally inappropriate. Rather than stats covering the ability to hit, run, throw, or field, the team's front office found that a player's ability to get on base was a much better predictor of how many runs he would score. So the Athletics recruited players with a high on-base percentage, paying less attention to stats, such as batting average. They went on to build a winning baseball team, and yes, on the cheap.

- Parents had an ongoing battle with their sixteen-year-old son, Eric, when it came to rousting him out of bed in the morning in order to make it to school on time. They eventually landed on the right motivating metric: his use of the car, beginning with weekends, was reduced every morning he was late getting ready for school.

- Rightfully recognizing that customer satisfaction was important to restaurant profitability and believing that low employee turnover was a favorable contributor to customer satisfaction, the managers of a national fast-food chain focused on retaining employees and reducing turnover. The executives were surprised at the data collected after the initiative was implemented: some restaurants with high employee turnover were in fact very profitable, while others with low turnover struggled. After a more thorough cause-and-effect analysis, the team learned that turnover among restaurant managers, not among lower-level employees, was the real driver. A shift in focus ultimately led to improved customer satisfaction and profitability.

- Wells Fargo Bank had, and still has, an appropriate strategy of building long-term customer relationships. In its 2016 annual report, the bank mentioned its effort to "best align our cross-sell metric with our strategic focus on long-term retail banking relationships." To track this, the bank measured and rewarded employees on the extent of cross-selling. The incentives, pressure to meet quotas, and the bank's sales culture led to well-publicized, perverse employee behavior, which has resulted in fines, fee reimbursements, and litigation accruals totaling close to $3.5 billion at last count, along with a loss of long-term customer relationships.

Whether in your role as a parent, a supervisor, or leader in an organization, you need to assess current metrics being used and take time to understand the steps needed to measure what truly matters. While each situation is admittedly unique, there are common considerations, as further described in this chapter. The following road map is designed to illustrate the links between strategic outcomes and the mission and shared vision for an organization. Metrics are typically relevant as integral parts of the scorecard and goals.

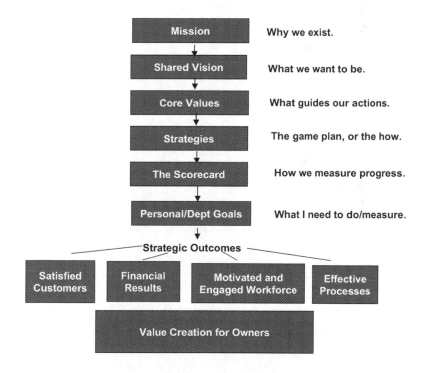

Step 1: Understand the Ultimate Objective. In the example above, it is economic value creation for the owners. It could be to maximize the longevity of the organization; or for a nonprofit, it could be related to lives impacted.

Step 2: Document the Drivers, Cause-and-Effect Based, Related to Achieving the Objective. For example, if satisfied customers is a key strategic outcome, one that helps drive value creation, then what are the drivers, financial and nonfinancial, long- versus short-term, and process-related that impact your customers? Examples may include timely responsiveness to issues, returns, product/service quality, product features versus competitors, value perception, delivery time, customer willingness to promote a product, etc.

Step 3: Develop Metrics for Each of the Drivers. The process of developing a list of around twenty-five key drivers should involve a facilitated brainstorming session. Recognize that top-level metrics are developed first and then the process is repeated to cascade it down to an individual performer level so that metrics are linked from the top to the bottom.

Characteristics of Good Metrics

- Use the SMART model—a metric should be specific, measurable, achievable, relevant, and time-based.
- The metrics should be balanced, meaning there must be a mix between financial and nonfinancial, process-oriented (predictive) results, long-term and short-term. Metrics should include some employee-based measures. Where appropriate, metrics should be captured in trend format versus just a point in time. And remember the fine print: past performance is no indication of future results. Hence, predictive metrics are important.
- Keep metrics simple and easy to understand, unlike the professional quarterback ratings, for example.
- Ensure that when isolated to a certain team, the factors are reliably controllable by them (e.g., revenue growth is not totally attributable to the sales team and is often impacted by things outside their control. Consider using accuracy of revenue projections as an alternative.)
- Research if the metrics are being used by competitors, recognizing that you are smarter than them, of course.

- Good metrics will:
  - o drive the right performance
  - o help in decision-making
  - o drive strategy
  - o highlight when something is not working
  - o provide focus and alignment from top to bottom

Common Errors/Misperceptions

These are potential pitfalls that should be avoided. Flawed metrics can destroy a business.

- Tying a metric to a bonus such that it creates unexpected or unwarranted behavior. For example, paying extra for the expedited delivery of pizza can lead to accidents or speeding tickets. It is best to relax a link between metrics and incentives.
- Use of vanity metrics, or ones that are convenient to measure and improve but do not say much about the underlying process related to goals you are trying to measure. Examples include website traffic that can look impressive but does not tell you much about the quality of the traffic or conversion rates. Page views is another measure that, considered alone, does not provide insights into whether users are finding valuable content or taking desired actions.
- Measuring the wrong driver or predictor (e.g., the Oakland Athletics example). Companies typically strive to maximize value over the long term, although earnings per share (EPS) is the most popular metric, along with sales revenue and sales growth. Research indicates that the causal relationship between sales growth and value creation is tenuous as is the EPS connection. The latter can be gamed by reducing amounts spent on preventive maintenance or new product development, suggesting that supplemental measures should also be monitored.

Suggestions

- Keep the number of metrics manageable—twenty-five max.
- Share results—trend data is helpful.
- Conduct periodic (six month) assessments of the metrics. Do they still measure what they originally intended to measure? Are they driving unacceptable behavior? Has the business changed, requiring new metrics?

Examples

See the following examples of various metrics, not all inclusive for sure:

Productivity:	Efficiency:
revenue per employee	expenses as a percentage of revenue
revenue per hour worked	process efficiency, such as the speed to deliver a package
average time to handle service requests	return on investment
units produced per hour or per day	Financial:
Quality:	variance to budget
failure rate	period-to-period expense or revenue variance
mean time between failures	monthly recurring revenue
defect rate	rate of return
product returns	net present value
customer opinion rating	payback period
Customer:	gross margin
share of wallet	earnings per share, or EBITDA
revenue per customer	run rate
customer satisfaction	Innovation:
loyalty	new products launched
customer complaints	new patents
churn rate	revenue from new products
acquisition costs	new ideas in the pipeline

2   LEADERSHIP/MANAGEMENT BASICS

This chapter covers the basics of effective leadership/management, which is simply the ability to influence individuals to willfully follow a direction, believe something, or act a certain way that is also in their best interests. In my opinion, *effective leadership* is the single most important factor related to the success or failure of an organization. And being credible and authentic serve as the critical foundation for an effective leader.

Our economy has changed significantly—from an industrial one, in which companies generated value primarily using tangible assets by transforming raw materials into finished products, to a knowledge-based one, in which value is created using intangible assets, including employee skills and capabilities combined with responsive business processes, databases, information systems, customer and vendor relationships, and innovative products or services. It has been estimated that intangible assets, not represented on a company's balance sheet, now represent more than 75 percent of the market capitalization of a company, with recorded, tangible net-book value (assets less liabilities) accounting for less than 25 percent, a reversal of the last century. So, the new reality is that people, human capital, must truly be treated as the most valuable asset in an organization.

Effective leadership is important to followers for several reasons:

Trust and respect: Trust and respect are the two most important and essential components of effective leadership. Leaders who are trustworthy and respectful of their followers' opinions and ideas can foster a positive work environment where individuals feel valued and appreciated. This can help build strong relationships between the leader and followers, leading to better communication, collaboration, and productivity.

Direction and guidance: A good leader provides direction and guidance to their followers. This helps followers understand what is expected of them, what their goals are, and how to achieve them. A clear vision and direction from a leader can help followers feel motivated and engaged in their work.

Support and encouragement: Effective leaders support and encourage their followers. This can be done through recognition of their achievements, providing resources to help them succeed, and offering constructive feedback. When followers feel supported and encouraged, they are more likely to feel empowered and motivated to achieve their goals.

Development and growth: Good leaders help their followers develop and grow, both personally and professionally. This can be done through training and development opportunities, mentoring, and coaching. When leaders invest in their followers' development, they are demonstrating that they believe in their potential and are committed to helping them reach their goals.

Overall, effective leadership is important to followers because it can help them feel motivated, engaged, empowered, and supported. Good leaders foster positive work environments, build strong relationships with their followers, and help individuals to develop and grow, both personally and professionally.

Role Model of an Effective Leader

So you may appropriately ask, "If I want to be an effective leader, what does he or she look like? Is there a role model?" In Jim Collins's research of 1,435 large companies for his book, *Good to Great*, only eleven had made the leap from good to great results and then sustained them for fifteen years. Collins wrote, "Compared to high-profile leaders with big personalities who make headlines and become celebrities, the good-to-great leaders seem to have come from Mars. Self-effacing, quiet, reserved, even shy—these leaders are a paradoxical blend of personal humility and professional will. They are more like Lincoln and Socrates than Patton or Caesar." Regarding this paradoxical mix, Collins goes on to say, "Humility alone, of course, is not enough to make a great leader. Equally important is ferocious resolve—an almost stoic determination to do whatever needs to be done to make the organization great. And that determination is often accompanied by a toughness and ruthlessness in pursuit of goals." Take note of this image, including the personal characteristics mentioned by Collins—a paradoxical mix of humility and ferocious resolve. I have included several other characteristics that I label as "pillars" and consider very important to being an effective leader.

Needs of Those Being Led

To be an effective leader, especially with respect to inspiring others, it is essential to understand the nature and needs of those being led. Several years ago, the Gallup Organization published an analysis of interviews of more than a million employees over a twenty-five-year period where people were asked hundreds of different questions on every conceivable aspect of the workplace. They found that measuring the strength of a workplace could be simplified to twelve questions. These questions reveal what truly unleashes motivation within employees and thus identifies what should be addressed by the leaders of an organization:

1. Do I know what is expected of me at work?
2. Do I have the equipment and materials to do my work right?
3. At work, do I have the opportunity to do what I do best every day?
4. In the last seven days, have I received praise for doing good work?
5. Does my supervisor or someone at work seem to care about me as a person?
6. Is there someone at work who encourages my development?
7. At work do my opinions seem to count?
8. Does the mission/purpose of my company make me feel my job is important?
9. Are my coworkers are committed to doing quality work?
10. Do I have a best friend at work?
11. In the last six months, has someone talked to me about my development?
12. This last year, have I had opportunities at work to learn and grow?

What it boils down to is that employees are inspired by:

- challenging and meaningful work, including clear expectations and clear direction;
- involvement and personal responsibility for results;
- opportunities to learn, grow, and advance;
- being in a trusting, caring environment; and
- a feeling of being a part of something that is worthwhile, a grand purpose.

These results are further reinforced by a 2004 study by the Hay Group (Lamb, McKee), a global management consultancy, who found that of seventy-five key components of employee satisfaction, the following are critical:

- Trust and confidence in top leadership was the single most reliable predictor of employee satisfaction.
- Effective communication by leadership in three critical areas was the key to winning employee trust and confidence:
  1. Helping employees understand the company's overall business strategy.
  2. Helping employees understand how they contribute to achieving key business objectives.
  3. Sharing information with employees on both how the company is doing and how an employee's own division is doing—relative to strategic business objectives.

Armed with this knowledge, an effective leader can take steps to inspire those he or she is leading.

Inspiration v. Motivation

It is important for a leader to understand a simple fact of human nature: people are intrinsically motivated beings. They go to work for two key reasons: to earn enough to support themselves and their families and to make a difference. While at work, they seek to understand how and why they are making a difference. Employees do not need motivation. They need inspiration, which is an inside-out approach to leadership that can be entirely self-sustaining, as employees strive to reach their full potentials.

Traits of Good v. Bad Bosses

Good Boss Traits:

Communication skills: A good boss should have excellent communication skills, including the ability to listen actively, provide feedback, and articulate their expectations and vision clearly.

Empathy: A good boss should be empathetic toward their employees, understanding their concerns and showing they care about their well-being.

Decision-making: A good boss should be decisive, able to make difficult decisions and take responsibility for their actions.

Trustworthiness: A good boss should be trustworthy, honest, and transparent, keeping their promises and following through on their commitments.

Leadership skills: A good boss should possess strong leadership skills, including the ability to inspire and motivate their employees, provide direction, and encourage growth.

Bad Boss Traits:

Poor communication: A bad boss may struggle with communication, including being unclear or inconsistent in their instructions, failing to provide feedback, or ignoring employee concerns.

Lack of empathy: A bad boss may be insensitive or dismissive toward employee concerns or needs, causing employees to feel undervalued or unsupported.

Indecisiveness: A bad boss may struggle with decision-making, avoiding difficult choices or being indecisive, leading to confusion and frustration among employees.

Unreliability: A bad boss may be unreliable, failing to keep their promises or follow through on commitments, causing employees to lose trust in their leadership.

Micromanagement: A bad boss may be overly controlling, micromanaging their employees' every move, causing stress and reducing productivity.

Overall, good bosses should possess strong communication, leadership, empathy, and decision-making skills, while bad bosses may struggle with these traits, leading to employee dissatisfaction and decreased productivity.

Management v. Leadership

There is often confusion related to the roles of *managers* versus *leaders*. Thus, before proceeding, it is important to address this potential confusion (or to add to it). In his book, *On Becoming a Leader*, Warren Bemis suggested the following:

- The manager administers; the leader innovates.
- The manager focuses on systems and structure; the leader focuses on people.
- The manager relies on control; the leader inspires trust.
- The manager has a short-range view; the leader has a long-range perspective.
- The manager asks how and when; the leader asks what and why.
- The manager has his or her eye on the bottom line; the leader's eye is on the horizon.
- The manager imitates; the leader originates.
- The manager accepts the status quo; the leader challenges it.
- The manager is the classic good soldier; the leader is his or her own person.
- The manager does things right; the leader does the right things.

The book was published in 1989, and it may be appropriate to question a few of the above, especially recognizing that we continue to move from the industrial age to the information age, where knowledge workers are vital. Both managers and leaders must focus on people and employee engagement. Nevertheless, the list serves the useful purpose of illustrating that managing and leading go hand-in-hand and both must be employed depending upon the circumstances or the stage in one's career.

Another more current perspective comes from Marcus Buckingham and Curt Coffman in their book, *First, Break All the Rules*:

> "Conventional wisdom is proud of maxims like 'Managers do things right. Leaders do the right things.' This demeans the manager's role. Great managers look inward—inside the company, into each individual, into the differences in style, goals, needs and motivation of each person. Great

leaders by contrast look outward—at the competition, out at the future, at alternative routes forward. Great managers are not mini-executives waiting for leadership to be thrust upon them. And great leaders are not simply managers who have developed sophistication. The core activities of each are simply different. If companies confuse the two roles by expecting every manager to be a leader, or if they define 'leader' as simply a more advanced form of 'manager,' then the important catalyst role will soon be undervalued, poorly understood, and poorly played, hurting the company."

John Kotter, Harvard, in his 1990 article, "What Leaders Really Do," suggests that management and leadership are different but complementary and that one cannot function without the other. Leaders, he proposes, prepare organizations for change and help them cope as they struggle through it, while managers cope with complexity.

Each employee will function as a leader in some circumstances and a manager in others. The higher up one goes in an organization, the more the shift in the mix of management/leadership roles, as hypothetically illustrated below:

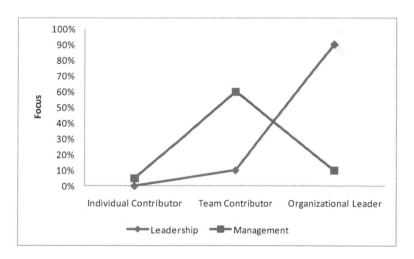

As a leader moves from an individual contributor to an organizational leader, his or her focus on leadership versus management responsibilities increases.

Leadership Levels

As the chart above implies, there are three levels of leadership, which one may progress through in his or her career, each having distinct characteristics:

Level 1: Individual Contributor
- in early stage of career
- relies on others for direction, feedback, and development
- exhibits personal leadership through functional and special project efforts, some of which may be team projects
- may be considered a functional expert
- may have ambition to move beyond this level
- possibly identified as a high-potential employee

Level 2: Team Leader
- provides direction to a team as a team lead or manager
- accomplishes results through others and holds others accountable
- coaches/develops others
- reinforces the culture through his/her actions
- performs a combination of management and leadership duties
- exhibits depth and breadth of technical/functional knowledge
- may have ambition or potential to become an organizational leader

Level 3: Organizational Leader
- top tier of the organization
- active in shaping the culture, including defining the metrics
- involved/influential in key decisions
- creates vision and strategic direction for his/her area of responsibility
- champions change efforts
- active in representing the organization and in outside networking
- sponsors leadership development and succession planning
- plays key role in internal and external communications

This notion of different levels of leadership is *important* because most authors, and most leadership-development programs, fail to recognize that there are different competencies relevant to each level. For example, strong strategic planning capabilities are critical for the organizational leader but generally of lesser importance for the individual contributor.

Key Roles

It is important to understand and buy into the key roles of a leader. This discussion and its balance will focus on the highest leadership level, the organizational leader. These are seven key leadership roles, in no particular order of importance:

1. Develop and communicate a shared vision/direction and goals.
2. Establish priorities and allocate resources.
3. Drive change and innovation.
4. Ensure organizational alignment, including implementation of appropriate processes such as strategic planning, performance management, rewards and recognition, etc., so the organization can be focused from top to bottom.
5. Solve problems, remove barriers, and make decisions.
6. Implement the culture through the tone at the top (via actions, metrics, and words).
7. Develop and inspire others to follow.

Since these are, for the most part, self-explanatory, there is no need to elaborate on each.

Key Functions

A leader needs, and accepts, three functions:

- authority—the right to make decisions
- responsibility—the assignment for achieving goals
- accountability—acceptance of success or failure

A leader needs all three to succeed. If given the responsibility and the accountability but not the authority, the leader will most likely fail.

Key Leadership Styles

Leadership styles are typically the patterns of behavior used to influence others. Each has its own strengths and weaknesses. The following describes the key styles:

1. **Servant leadership**: Servant leaders prioritize the needs of their team members over their own and focus on empowering and supporting them to achieve their goals. They prioritize listening, empathy, and support, often taking a coaching or mentoring role. Team members are viewed as assets of the organization. The organization chart is essentially turned upside down, with more importance given to those who are closest to the market and the customers. This leadership style can be highly effective in fostering trust, collaboration, and a positive work environment. However, it can also lead to challenges in decision-making as the focus on meeting the needs of team members may sometimes conflict with the goals of the organization.

2. **Autocratic leadership**: Autocratic leaders make decisions independently, without consulting their teams. They exercise complete control over their team and expect them to follow direction without question. Team members are viewed as a commodity. This style can be effective in situations where quick, decisive action is required, such as in a crisis or emergency situation. However, it can create a negative work environment as team members may feel undervalued or demotivated by the lack of involvement and decision-making authority.

3. **Democratic leadership**: Democratic leaders involve their teams in the decision-making process, soliciting input and feedback before making a decision. This style fosters a collaborative and creative environment as team members feel empowered and involved. However, it can also slow down decision-making because input from multiple sources may lead to conflicting opinions or viewpoints.

4. **Laissez-faire leadership**: Laissez-faire leaders provide minimal direction or guidance, allowing team members to work independently and make decisions on their own. This style can be effective in situations where team members are highly skilled and

motivated as it allows them to take ownership of their work and be creative. However, it can lead to confusion and disorganization because team members may not have clear direction.

5. **Transformational leadership**: Transformational leaders inspire and motivate their teams to achieve their goals, through a combination of vision, charisma, and individualized attention. They focus on developing their team member's skills and competencies, while empowering them to take ownership of their work. This style can be highly effective in fostering innovation, creativity, and high-performance teams. However, it can also lead to burnout, as transformational leaders may expect their team to work long hours and sacrifice personally time for the sake of the team or organization.

Styles can be situation specific, and thus a combination of the above is often employed depending on the circumstances (e.g., autocratic in a crisis).

The Pillars of Effective Leadership

My experience suggests that there are three pillars of effective leadership, each having specific attributes, competencies, or approaches that if exhibited and/or implemented will enable, but not guarantee, that you can be an effective leader. The pillars, labeled *Be, Know,* and *Do* are borrowed from the US army's leadership manual, supplemented by my fifty-five years of experience. As explained further, being credible and authentic is the foundation for an effective leader.

Pillar #1. What You Need to *BE*

This pillar is primarily about your character or personal behavior—those attributes and values that are manifestations of motives and actions, such as being:

- **Authentic**: As the cartoon character Popeye often said, "I yam what I yam, and that's all what I yam." Authentic leaders are comfortable with themselves, passionate, and unafraid to admit mistakes. Several of the following attributes contribute to authenticity.

- **Credible**: Being authentic assumes being credible, as evidenced by unwavering integrity. Credibility and authenticity form the foundation of an effective leader and are *absolutely required* for others to want to follow you willingly and enthusiastically. Without credibility and authenticity, you will struggle to earn the respect of the people you lead.
- **A coach**: Being empathetic, caring, magnanimous (giving credit where it is due), connecting with people, serving them, and helping them succeed are essential to building trust and respect.
- **Courageous**: This means being bold and willing to take reasonable, calculated risks, persevering in tough times and making tough decisions
- **Self-Assured**: You must be emotionally stable, displaying confident calmness under pressure, having a positive self-image, and showing little or no need for approval. You may have a strong, but not big, ego, blaming yourself before pointing the finger at others.
- **Intuitive/creative**: This means seeing what others cannot, thinking outside the box and helping others do so. These represent the visionary, forward-looking traits of a leader.
- **Driven/passionate for results**: Being competitive, decisive, focused, and assertive will help ensure a clear understanding of expectations and direction. Always ask, "How can we do things better?"
- **Analytical**: Having the ability to look at situations, synthesize multidimensional data, and confront reality quickly is key.
- **Inspirational**: You should exude optimism, genuine enthusiasm, excitement, and energy to achieve results. This is different from motivation, which comes from within.
- **Adaptable**: Are you open to change, input, and challenges? Do you listen to understand?
- **Forward looking**: This means having the ability to see and define a better future (being a visionary), recognizing patterns and new possibilities, instilling a belief in tomorrow. You are able

to articulate a vision of the future and connect employees' values and needs with those of the organization.

- **Presentable**: You earn respect by dressing appropriately and being groomed for the situation while understanding and employing acceptable social etiquette (e.g., introductions, meals, internet, etc.)

Since credibility and authenticity have been identified as the foundations of a leader, they deserve more attention. Lack of either is a fatal flaw. Followers want a credible, authentic leader and will go with them enthusiastically and willingly, not because they have to. The notion of credibility and authenticity assumes competency, which is having the ability to get things done, a proven track record, and some technical skills. Most importantly, however, it is about earning trust and respect by:

- keeping promises
- communicating honestly about how you feel and why
- erring on the side of fairness
- doing what you say you are going to do, when you say you will do it
- being consistent in your actions, walking the talk
- recognizing that no lie is small enough to not matter

Sounds a lot like honesty and integrity, doesn't it? It is, and it is the foundation to leadership. You may also recognize the importance of these actions in raising children.

Pillar #2. What You Need to *Know*

These are the special competencies, skills, knowledge, or talents employed:

- *Hiring, developing, retaining, and separating people*: You must have the ability to establish systems to attract, retain, and develop talented individuals and surround yourself with the *right* people, oftentimes smarter than you, employing them in the right roles and continually developing them. This also implies an ability release those who do not fit.
- *Exceptional analysis / problem-solving skills*: You should be able to gather diverse inputs, synthesize them, and view the situation/ organization systemically, discerning cause-and-effect relationships

and discovering root causes plus coherent patterns, often within incoherent or incomplete data.

- *Unemotional decision-making*: You should have the capability to make sound, timely, and unemotional decisions, standing by them once made, even if circumstances cause course corrections later.
- *Ability to prioritize*: You should be able to <u>prioritize actions</u> exceptionally with incomplete data and manage time effectively.
- *Organizational savvy*: You should have a clear understanding of the industry and the organization's business model.
- *Use change management effectively*: You should have knowledge of the change-management process and the ability to use it effectively.
- *Effective listening abilities*: Listening skills and the ability to ask intelligent, thoughtful questions will reinforce humility and your own intelligence.
- *Communication skills*: You need good verbal, written, and presentation abilities, in order to engage others and manage conflict.
- *International awareness*: You should have global awareness, understanding, and, preferably, actual experience in a foreign country.

Pillar #3. What You Need to *DO*

Performance/execution—the following are actions you can take to achieve success:

- *Exhibit high standards*: Establish high expectations for yourself and others, using a handful of standards of excellence and holding all accountable.
- *Live the values*: Define, live, and exemplify the core values of the organization. Be the role model.
- *Demonstrate consistency and fairness*: Act with courage, consistency, and fairness in applying the rules or making decisions.
- *Focus on people*: Surround yourself with the best people by hiring, developing, promoting, and rewarding high performers while taking prompt action related to those who are not performing or do not fit.

- *Over communicate*: Communicate openly and honestly; repeat yourself a lot.
- *Demonstrate effective resource utilization*: Allocate, acquire, and deploy resources effectively (capital, people, time).
- *Treat failures as stepping stones to success*: Uniquely handle failures as learning opportunities.
- *Pick appropriate metrics and hold people accountable*: Choose the right metrics—ones that drive results, hold people accountable, and shape the culture.
- *Be a change agent*: Drive change and innovation.
- *Be clear and focused*: Instill clarity in the organization regarding who it serves, its core strengths, the key metric(s), and what actions/changes should be implemented.

Summing It Up—Being an Effective Leader

The ideal effective leader possesses and exhibits the character traits described above, has a good grasp of special competencies, and effectively executes the actions identified. While no one can be perfect with respect to employing the Be-Know-Do characteristics of an effective leader, personal introspection and self-awareness can help identify strengths and weakness, leading to the determination and implementation of ongoing leadership development and improvement plans. Remember that "knowledge is potential." Personal motivation is the spark that will put knowledge into *action*, benefitting you and those you lead.

Remember too that as a leader, in the final analysis, what is most important is that *leading is primarily about them, those you are leading, not you!*

3 EFFECTIVE COMMUNICATION

The Basics

Effective communication, both oral and written, is a critical competency for success in all aspects of life. Here are some guiding principles for improving communication:

1. **Clarity**: It is essential to be clear in your communication, whether oral or written. Ensure that your message is easy to understand and avoids jargon, be it technical or company-related, that your audience may not be familiar with.
2. **Brevity**: Keep communication brief and to the point. Avoid using long, convoluted sentences and unnecessary details that may confuse or bore your audience.
3. **Audience awareness**: Understand your audience and tailor your communication to their needs and preferences. This involves understanding their backgrounds, interests, and communication styles (e.g., verbal, written, data focused, etc.).
4. **Listening**: Be an active listener. Effective communication is a two-way process that involves listening and speaking or writing. It is important to be attentive and responsive to your audience and clarify any misunderstandings to ensure that your message is received and understood.
5. **Context**: Consider the setting, the purpose of your communication, and any cultural or social norms that may impact it. Effective communication involves a complex interplay of verbal and nonverbal elements, and the relative importance of each can vary widely depending on the situation and individuals involved. It is a common belief that 55 percent of communication is via body

language and 38 percent is tied to tone of voice, although these are based on a limited context and thus not universally applicable.

6. **Feedback**: Seek feedback on your communication and be open to constructive criticism.

Following these guiding principles will enable you to improve your oral and written communication to more effectively convey your message.

As a supplement to these guiding principles, the following is an English grammar overview highlighting common errors in communication, the application of which may impact the perception of you by others.

- *assure* v. *ensure* v. *insure*: Although each of these has to do with "making an outcome sure," the terms are not interchangeable. To *assure* means to say what's what to people and promise or say with confidence. To *ensure* means to make certain that something happens. To *insure* means to protect things against a risk, for example by paying an insurance company.
- *alright* v. *all right*: This is a spelling issue. Just remember that *alright* is not *all right.*
- *affect* v. *effect*: *Affect* is usually a verb that means to influence or change. *Effect* is a noun and is the result of change. *The effect of the virus was major. The rain affected my disposition.*
- *between* v. *among*: *Between* refers to two things that are clearly separated, while *among* refers to things that are not clearly separated. *You choose between your black dress and white one. You walk among your friends.*
- commas: These are a few rules related to the use of commas:
  o Use a comma after an introductory phrase in a sentence or an introductory word such as *however.*
  o Use one between two independent clauses joined by a conjunction such as *and, or, but, so,* etc.
- *complement* v. *compliment*: While these are pronounced the same, they have very different meanings. *Compliment* is an expression of praise and can be used as a noun or a verb. You can *compliment* your friends new dress or you can pay someone a *compliment.* The other, *complement*, means to enhance or complete something. The wine selection *complements* the meal, or the carpet *complements* the color of the walls.

- *dangling modifiers*: These happen when a descriptive phrase does not apply to the noun that immediately follows it. *After increasing for months, Jon finally decided to invest in the market. Jon finally decided to invest in the market after seeing it increase for months.*

- *espresso* v. *expresso*: *Expresso* is a misspelling of *espresso*, a form of coffee.

- *farther* v. *further*: These are typically misused words intended to mean "at a greater distance." However, the word *farther* is the appropriate one when referring to physical distances, while *further* is used to refer to figurative, nonphysical distances. *New York is farther away than Chicago. The company has fallen further away from its revenue goal.*

- *himself* v. *hisself*: Himself is a pronoun used to reference a male who has been previously mentioned in the text. Hisself is deemed grammatically incorrect and rarely used in formal writing.

- *"I couldn't care less"* v. *"I could care less"*: Both mean not concerned or interested at all, with the latter being rejected by most grammarians.

- *i.e.* v. *e.g.*: These are easily confused. *i.e.* means "that is," while *e.g.* means "for example."

- *regardless* v. *irregardless*: While a word, *irregardless* is a nonstandard expression that should be avoided.

- *its* v. *it's*: *It's* is a contraction for "it is," while *its* is a possessive form of *it*, which stands for inanimate things or ideas, and is used to indicate possession, ownership, belonging, etc.

- *less* v. *fewer*: Use *fewer* for things that are quantifiable or can be counted. Use *less* when discussing things that are not quantifiable. While the sign in the grocery checkout aisle says, "10 Items or Less," that statement is actually incorrect as it should read *fewer*.

- *me* v. *I*: This is a challenging one. Consider the incorrect sentence: "Email the report to Eric and I." Now take "Eric and" out, which would make it read, "Email the report to I." Obviously, the correct word to use is *me*, which technically is the object of the sentence.

- *much* v. *many*: *Many* modifies things that can be counted, while *much* modifies things that cannot be counted. *Much* tends to modify singular nouns

- *of* v. *have*: You have heard *woulda*, *shoulda*, or *coulda* and mistakenly assumed they mean "would of," "should of," or "could of." In reality, the second word is not *of* but *have*. So, it is more appropriate to say *would've*, *should've*, or *could've*.

- *"of utmost importance"* v. *"of upmost importance"*: *Upmost* is a shortening of *uppermost*, meaning the top of a stack or ranking. Utmost, on the other hand, means to the greatest extent possible or highest degree.

- *possessive nouns*: People often make mistakes when deciding where to put an apostrophe. If a noun is plural, add the apostrophe after the *s*. *All the dogs' ears perked up.* If a noun is singular but ends in *s*, also put the apostrophe after the *s* such as *the dress's bright colors.* However, if the noun is singular and does not end in an *s*, then add an apostrophe and add the *s*. *The dog's ears perked up.*

- *seen* v. *saw*: The word *seen* is typically misused and could clearly demonstrate your lack of understanding of proper English. *"I seen my friend at the store"* is incorrect. *Seen* is always used with have, has, had, is, was, will be, had been, etc. *I had seen my friend at the store.* The word *seen* must never follow directly after I, she, he, we, they, Jon (any person's name). *Saw* is used after these words, such as *I saw my friend at the store.*

- *separate* v. *seperate*: *Separate* is one of the most misspelled words in the English language. It is easier to remember the difference if you consider that the word *separate* has an *a* in it and means "pull apart" (*apart* beginning with an *a*). *Seperate* is a misspelling and should be avoided.

- *supposedly* v. *supposably or supposively*: *Supposedly* means allegedly. The word is often misused when one usually intends to say supposedly but instead says supposably.

- *take* v. *bring*: The use of *bring* or *take* depends upon your point of reference. You ask people to *bring* things to you. You *take* things to the place you are going. In other words, you *bring* things here and *take* things there.

- *themselves* v. *theirselves*: *Theirselves* is a marker of poor English and seldom used. Themselves refers to a group of people, animals, or objects previously mentioned.

- *then* v. *than*: The word *than* is used to make comparisons: "My home is bigger than yours." *Then* is an adverb used to situate actions related to time.

- *to v. too*: *To* typically describes a destination or recipient. "I sent the email *to* my boss." *Too* on the other hand is used as an alternative of *also* or *as well*. "Jason, too, is an IU grad." Note the commas before and after *too*. When using the word *too* in the middle of a sentence, the general rule is to use a comma both before and after. No need for a comma when too is the last word in a sentence.

- *use of a colon*: Use a colon to introduce an item or series of items. Think of it as a substitute for *namely* or *that is*. Generally, never capitalize the first item after a colon unless it is a proper noun, a full sentence, or if the information following the colon requires two or more complete sentences. However, if the list is comprised of bullet points or phrases preceded by letter, it is okay to capitalize the items.

- *use of semicolons*: A semicolon is typically used to link two independent clauses that are closely related. You may also use a semicolon between items in a list or series if any of the items contain commas.

- *who* v. *whom*: Use *whom* when referring to the object of the verb. Remember it this way: If you can replace the word with *he* or *she*, use *who*. If you can replace it with *him* or *her*, or if it used as the object of a verb or preposition, use *whom*. *Who/whom* is in charge? She is in charge. Therefore, *who* is appropriate. To *who/whom* should I speak? *Whom* is correct since it is the object.

MAKING EFFECTIVE PRESENTATIONS

While Microsoft PowerPoint is currently the most popular software for presentations, few of us know the key principles of making an effective presentation when using it or similar products. Before you jump headlong into the details of this chapter, I ask that you step back and discard all existing perceptions. One of my favorite sayings is, "No one is completely worthless; you can always serve as a bad example." I have been there and done that, and I suspect that, unknowingly, you have done the same, potentially hurting your opportunity to progress in an organization. I ask that you trust me and work on implementing as many of the suggestions in this chapter as possible, despite the fact that some may seem to be outside your comfort zone. Most people treat the slides in a presentation as if they are notes to read and not tools to help convey data or persuade others to action. So the learning objectives of this chapter include enabling you to become a professional presenter; enhancing your ability to make an impressive, engaging, and interactive presentation; and increasing career opportunities.

Preparation

In developing your presentation, it is essential that you take into account the following factors, some of which can be addressed in order, to enhance its quality:

- Know your audience—their roles, education, and knowledge level.
- Clearly understand the purpose of your presentation. Is it to convey data or to persuade, taking the audience from point A to your objective, point B?
- Consider the setting and the time of day. (Right after lunch is tough.)
- Are you the only presenter and thus providing the key messages?
- Identify three or four things you want them to leave with and the WIIFT (what's in it for them).
- Force yourself to prepare the three *P*s—the *purpose* of the presentation, the *process* you will use—such as ten slides followed by a question-and-answer section—and the *product* of the

presentation, which will cause you to identify what you consider to be the expected outcomes (a decision, better understanding, identification of next steps, etc.).

- Prepare an outline to assist you in developing the appropriate flow.

Slide Tips

- Recognize perception psychology and human predispositions, such as the fact our eyes jump to the upper left corner of a slide first and then sweep to the right. This is known as a reflexive cross sweep. By being aware of this instinctive reaction, you can minimize the use of excessive graphics, thus reducing eye sweeps.
- Keep slides simple.
- Limit the number of words, and, if possible, avoid bullet points. The audience should be listening, not reading.
- Use high quality graphics.
- Use grammatically correct parallelism, meaning each line begins with a verb or each begins with a noun.
- Use indentations for subpoints and try to use a maximum of only one.
- Use professional fonts and don't use more than three different ones.
- Recognize some in the audience may be color-blind, meaning they have difficulty distinguishing between shades of red, yellow, and green.
- Check the vertical alignment of your text/lines to ensure there are no extraneous spaces.
- For longer presentations, use a separator slide between sections (a one-line slide describing the next section).
- Limit the use of punctuation, especially exclamation points and periods.
- Use proportional spacing for a professional look.
- Ideally, force yourself to use a five-by-six pattern—five lines down and up to six words across, although this can be a challenge. If you have more than five points to make, build them one at a time on succeeding slides.

- Add some pizzazz by putting text in a box and enhancing the box's lines or employing a "reverse out" by changing the background color and the font.
- Create a consistent look and feel and maintain it throughout.
- Be consistent in your choice of font and in your choice of case.
- Keep font size to a minimum of twenty-four to twenty-eight points.
- Avoid abbreviations or contractions.
- Add some shadows and bolding to make text more legible.
- Use sharp contrast, such as light text on a dark background or vice versa.
- While it is okay to insert your company logo, minimize the size. Consider using it as a watermark with a subtle, embossed effect.
- Avoid the clutter caused by a recurring "Company Confidential" warning on every side, slogans, or copyright notice.
- Use a lot of blank space.

What to Avoid and Typical Presentation Issues

While the previous section highlighted helpful tips, it is important to consider things to avoid, such as:

- overly detailed slides with extraneous punctuation, bullets, etc.
- illogical flow
- too long
- no clarification of benefits to the audience—the "what's in it for them" (WIIFT)
- a monotone voice
- bullets (use summarized thoughts versus complete sentences)
- sound effects
- clip art
- flashy slide transitions as they can detract from the points you are making
- reading directly from the presentation
- telling jokes (This can distract from your message.)
- using the slides as a handout
- excessive graphics (less is more)

- two-line titles
- subtitles (use a dot, not a dash, if you do use them)
- apostrophe and *s* for plurals since this context is for contractions (two Nates are here or Nate's here)
- more than three font styles

Delivery

Tell them about what you are going to tell them, then tell them, then summarize by telling them what you just told them, including a call to action. State up front how long your presentation will be and a brief agenda of what will be covered. Consider beginning with an opening from one of the following:

- a question directed at members of the audience
- a factoid, such as a striking statistic or little-known fact
- a look forward or backward
- a short human-interest story or anecdote
- a quotation or endorsement from a respected source
- an aphorism or familiar saying—e.g., "the whole is greater than the sum of its parts"
- an analogy, mentioning two seemingly unrelated items that help illuminate a complex or obscure topic

When presenting:

- remember to view your presentation through the eyes of the audience, addressing their needs and your goals
- deliberately speak slowly
- raise and lower your voice during the presentation, avoiding a monotonous, sleep-inducing voice
- vary the length of your sentences
- pause occasionally
- focus on WIIFT (what's in it for them)
- make eye contact with people in the audience for an extended period of time.

Suggestion

I have saved the best advice for last. This is an approach that has worked well for me. Develop the PowerPoint "Notes" section of each slide first, recognizing that while many of the above principles still apply, you can be more verbose, descriptive, and/or prescriptive in this section. Preparing this first makes it much easier to summarize your points on the main slides. And if you want to provide handouts, the "Notes" pages are an ideal way for someone to grasp your messages.

LISTENING EFFECTIVELY

"If we were supposed to talk more than we listen, we would have two tongues and one ear."
—Mark Twain

Effective listening is a life skill not generally taught but critically important to one's success in every interpersonal exchange. As with most skills, there are key principles or best practices that apply, and practicing these is the key to becoming an effective active listener. Listening is not the same as hearing, the latter being a physical process that happens automatically. Listening, on the other hand, requires the listener be as engaged in the process as is the speaker. It also requires one to focus not only on the story/ words being said but also observing nonverbal cues, the use of language and voice, how the message is being told, and what is left unsaid or only partially said. Thus, your ability to listen effectively, and actively, depends upon the degree to which you perceive and understand more than just the words.

Listening Principles

- Consciously zip your lips when someone else is talking. Suppress the urge to interrupt and be comfortable with periods of silence.
- Focus first on what is being said and how it is being said rather than formulating ways to respond, which is the biggest challenge for anyone because while average speech rates are between 125 and 175 words per minute, we can process between 400 and 800 words, leaving plenty of time to daydream or think of a response. Fight the urge!
- Maintain eye contact with the speaker, but don't stare, in order to demonstrate that you are listening and understanding. This takes practice but is very helpful.
- Wait and watch for nonverbal cues—gestures, facial expressions, and eye movements.
- Nod occasionally to signal that you are understanding.
- Interrupt to clarify a point. Restating what was just said is helpful (e.g., using "it sounds as if ..." or "what you are saying is ...").

- Ask expansive "what" and "how" questions, which prompt speakers to feel listened to.
- Put away the phone to eliminate electronic distractions.
- Practice, practice, practice! Asking a friend, spouse, or coworker to provide feedback regarding how your listening ability is perceived or has improved is also helpful.

It is important to be competent in using various process tools, whether in business or personally. One that will enable you to stand out and excel is the ability to run effective meetings.

Running an Effective Meeting

Meetings play a crucial role in organizations because they facilitate communication, collaboration, and decision-making among team members. Through meetings, team members can discuss project progress, share ideas, and brainstorm solutions to challenges faced by the organization. Meetings also help in establishing clear goals and objectives, assigning tasks, and tracking progress. They allow team members to provide feedback, raise concerns, and identify areas that need improvement. Moreover, meetings promote team building and foster a sense of community within the organization. Therefore, it is essential for organizations to schedule regular meetings to keep everyone on the same page and ensure that the organization is functioning effectively and efficiently.

In any organization, meeting purposes may fall into one of the following: (1) problem solving, (2) influencing others, (3) making decisions, and (4) sharing information. As most attest, many meetings are not run effectively or efficiently, and in many cases, there are too many. The following offers basic tips and tools for you to improve meetings in your organization.

Planning

What applies to effective meetings can be characterized by the tried-and-true seven *P*s developed by the British army—proper prior planning and preparation prevents piss-poor performance.

The first step is clearly understanding and documenting the purpose of the meeting—what do you want to accomplish? With this in mind, an agenda or list of what is needed should be created to achieve the purpose of the meeting. The agenda needs to include an introductory chart (see recommended 3-P chart that follows) and a summary that details the next steps if appropriate. Allocate time for each agenda item, preferably limiting the total time to one hour. Half- or full-day events are an exception.

You know how best to sequence items on the agenda based on the meeting's purpose. Selecting the right people to invite is also dependent on the purpose to include both key decision-makers and impacted implementers.

Once prepared, the draft agenda should be distributed to invitees, preferably a week in advance and should include the purpose of the meeting. You may want to ask the attendees if they have any questions or additional items to add since allowing them to contribute will ensure they feel like an important part of the process.

It is helpful if your organization adopts meeting guidelines, a draft of which follows for potential use. These guidelines help provide some discipline and focus for participants.

Guidelines

- Agendas will be issued in advance and specify whether a presentation is for information or requires a decision. The agenda should specify what, if anything, each attendee is to bring.
- Meetings will begin on time.
- Presentations must have a 3-P (purpose, process, and product) chart and ideally should be distributed in advance.
- For information-only topics, presenters should assume that the audience has read the material in advance. Accordingly, the presenter should cover only key points or charts/graphs that may

need additional explanation. Presenters should avoid reading word charts, recognizing that the audience can do so at a faster rate.

- For decision topics, following the discussion regarding the decision, the presenter or sponsor of the topic will concisely summarize what he or she heard regarding the decision/direction.
- The organizer will identify an official notetaker and timekeeper, the latter serving as an official devil's advocate.
- Presenters should stick to the time allocated for the topic, which will include time for discussion. Excessive discussion beyond the control of the presenter will be forgiven.
- The meeting facilitator or designee is empowered to ensure presentations and discussion stay focused on the topic (but he or she should capture any important follow-up items for subsequent discussion).
- Participants are expected to complete assigned prework (e.g., reading, data gathering).
- Presenters should maintain a visible parking lot of issues requiring follow-up and/or issues not relevant to the meeting's purpose.
- The objectives of interactions during a meeting will be problem-solving, learning, collaboration, and decision-making, not fault finding.
- Participants will be disciplined in the use of time, adhering to the agenda and scheduled breaks.
- There will be no checking emails, surfing the web, or replying to texts during the meeting.
- Participants will listen, communicate candidly, yet tactfully, and ask questions for clarification.
- Key points, decisions, assignments, and due dates will be summarized at the end.
- Minutes following a meeting will not rehash the presentation but instead reflect decisions and agreed upon follow-ups, including names and dates.

Note: These guidelines are intended to improve the effectiveness and efficiency of meetings, which will allow for either adding agenda items or freeing up time for other value-added activities. Until everyone understands them, make sure they are placed on the table in front of each participant.

Kickoff

If you get nothing else from this white paper, adopting meeting guidelines and using the following as the introductory 3-P chart for all meetings will go a long way toward improving the efficiency and effectiveness of your meetings.

3-P Overview

purpose(s): Why I am presenting? Is this informational or does it require a decision?

process: How will present the material and what are my expectations regarding discussion (e.g., advance distribution of key material; PowerPoint presentation; hold questions until the end; decisions will be made based on majority vote or group consensus or leader decides)?

product(s): What do I want the audience to leave with (e.g., a better understanding of X or recommendations related to Y)?

Tips on Handling Typical Meeting Issues On-Site

Dominant Participant: If one person seems to dominate the discussion, you may:

- thank him or her for the input and call on someone else;
- walk closer to the individual, which helps draw attention to you and away from the dominant participant; or
- during a break, ask the person to jot down their thoughts and allow others to contribute.

Late Arrivers/Early Departures:

- consistently start your meetings on time, which will establish respect for your focused approach

- to preempt early departures, ask the group if everyone can stay for the entire designated time
- after the meeting, follow up with those arriving late or leaving early to understand the underlying cause for their behavior, thus sending a message

Interruptions or Deviations from the Meeting Purpose:

- refer to the 3-P chart displayed
- capture deviations as parking lot items
- refer to the meeting guidelines, which cover the ground rules for a meeting. They should be placed on the table in advance of the meeting.
- call for a break

Virtual Meetings

While webinars and Go-To Meeting software has been in use for some time, the corona-virus pandemic accelerated the work from home trend, which necessitates an increased number of virtual meetings. Such meetings create the additional challenge of keeping participants engaged.

These are guidelines intended to enable an effective meeting while encouraging participation of those involved in a remote, virtual setting:

- Ideally, use video conference software for your meeting, thus minimizing the opportunity for a participant to hide or engage in other activities during the meeting. Research indicates that 55 percent of communication is via body language and another 38 percent is tied to tone of voice, therefore it is helpful to use video conferencing as your medium.
- Give attendees a task to either involve them in the discussion or encourage them to listen closely. For example, tell participants that you expect each of them to report at the end of the meeting on some key point or assign one to take notes and another to document any questions or issues. It helps to assign one to call a time-out or create a parking lot item when the discussion deviates from the agenda.

- Follow the tips included in the section covering "effective presentations," especially guidance on limiting the number of slides.
- Recognize that remote team members may not know each other in the same way those who work in an office know and interact with each other. Hence, it may be important to create some team-building exercises over time in advance of virtual meetings. Also consider engaging in some small talk at the beginning of a meeting to build trust and rapport.
- Like for an onsite meeting, you should create a clear agenda.
- Meeting guidelines should be modified to include the following:
  - o expectations on what each attendee is to contribute
  - o details on the process to provide input during the meeting
  - o cameras on
  - o muted phones
  - o no interrupting others when they are speaking
  - o no working on other tasks during the meeting
- Have everyone introduce themselves.
- Ensure everyone contributes. Consider having each provide insight on the topic before ending the meeting (helps involve the introverts).
- Summarize assignments, issues, due dates, etc., at the conclusion of the meeting.
- Ask attendees how the next meeting can be improved.

Follow-Up

Following a meeting, be it virtual or on-site, the organizer should send a brief summary highlighting decisions, assignments/responsibilities, and due dates, where applicable. Ideally, the memo will detail the what, the how, the who, and the when as well as the timing of the next meeting.

BRAINSTORMING

Certain meetings require ideation or creativity. Having knowledge of tools to facilitate such meetings is important to their efficiency and effectiveness. Brainstorming is a group creativity-facilitation process that everyone should have in his or her toolbox. Developed in the 1940's, the process enables a team to effectively and efficiently identify issues, prioritize solutions, develop strategic plans, and unleash creativity by spontaneously generating ideas. It is widely used by most Silicon Valley start-ups and is designed to be fast and flowing in an unrestrained way.

The following steps/guidelines assume that you are the one designated to facilitate a brainstorming session.

- Make sure you have a charter or purpose for the session.
- Ideally, there should be three to five people involved as this is a good size to ensure active participation.
- Provide a sufficient supply of Post-it notes, stick-on dots, and pens.
- Review the purpose of the session, the sponsor, and the deliverable, which should be written on a board or flip chart.
- Get buy-in and understanding from participants related to the meeting/brainstorming ground rules and process such as:
    o No input will be judged. This is a free-flow, unrestrained ideation process.
    o Verbally mention your input and then write it on a Post-it note. The purpose of describing your input is to stimulate the thinking of others.
    o Input will be taken for x minutes after which Post-it notes will be placed on the board or wall.
    o Two of you will be asked to review the input and arrange the Post-it notes into common themes or ideas.
    o The common ideas will be reviewed with the group, who will have the opportunity to provide any additional input.
    o For initial ranking of ideas, each will get five dots to place on the ideas that he or she feels is most compelling.
    o Final prioritization, if required, will be left to the executive sponsor of the session.

- As you begin a session, it is important to pose questions that force participants to take a new and unfamiliar perspective. Using a challenge question, such as "in what way?" can be helpful in spurring creativity.
- Make sure you capture and display every idea.
- Be sure to encourage wild or seemingly absurd ideas in the spirit of suspending judgment. Go for quantity, not quality.
- Do not include the boss as part of the group, since it can make participants hesitant to express unproven ideas—or have an excuse to be lazy. Subject matter experts can squelch new ideas because everyone defers to their presumed superior wisdom, even if they are biased or have incomplete knowledge of the issue at hand.

Recognize that this is an ideation tool. Make it work for your specific circumstances.

NEGOTIATING

The ability to effectively negotiate is a skill, an important tool for success in business and life in general. It requires discipline, perseverance, practice, preparation, and adherence to a process and set of guiding principles as outlined in this chapter. While part of an organization, your participation in negotiations may be limited, but at some point, it will be helpful to be knowledgeable of the key principles that are transferrable, like selling your house or purchasing a vehicle.

First, it is helpful to understand BATNA, which stands for "Best Alternative to a Negotiated Agreement." It is a concept first mentioned in the 1981 book *Getting to Yes: Negotiating Agreement without Giving In* by American marketing experts Roger Fisher, William Ury, and Bruce Patton. The term refers to the most advantageous alternative course of action a party can take if negotiations fail and an agreement cannot be reached. Depending on the situation, an alternative may be a cessation of negotiations, transition to another negotiating partner, court action, strikes, or the formation of other alliances. A negotiator should generally not accept a worse resolution than his or her BATNA. The best negotiators get to "yes" by being clear about what their alternatives are if they do not get a deal.

It is equally as important to know our counterpart's BATNA since by knowing it, we can potentially have a better understanding of what the ZOPA (Zone of Possible Agreement) of the negotiation will be.

The target is what you think is reasonably possible to get out of a negotiation. However, you should never reveal your target at the beginning of any negotiation, because your counterpart will typically never agree with your first proposal. After the first offer, negotiators need to make concessions because they enable the parties to move toward the ZOPA and demonstrate the intention to bargain in good faith. However, for concessions to work properly, they need to be clearly labeled and accompanied by an expectation that the other party will reciprocate with a willingness of meeting in the middle.

Perhaps as important as understanding negotiating principles is to recognize and avoid two basic mistakes:

- focusing too much on yourself rather listening to the other side
- telling the other party what you think your target is

The principles of negotiating include the following:

1. Prepare Rigorously

While most of us are predisposed to jumping right in, like painting a room for example, rigorous preparation will increase the probability of a favorable outcome.

Step one is to define and understand your BATNA and the ZOPA (described above). At the same time, you should assess the strengths and weaknesses of the person you will be negotiating with, including making sure he or she has decision-making/binding commitment authority. This may require consulting with others who have knowledge of the negotiating style or pattern of the individual you will be sitting across the table from. This data/perception gathering will enable you to learn some personal aspects of the other party, recognizing the importance of building rapport and earning their trust. Research all aspects of the negotiating topic and prepare a list of the potential WIIFM (what's in it for me) of both sides. Having more information than the other party may increase your negotiating power.

2. Develop Strategies

You should spend time developing strategies, including potential responses and/or contingency plans. First, however, recognize that you will never get what you want if you do not ask for it. Hence, the first offer is the most important one since it will be the benchmark by which the following offers will be compared. It may prove helpful to have a "back-pocket" giveaway in mind that will not hurt your negotiating position. Consider adding extras, such as nice-to-have features that may not be critical to the project/subject at hand but can be taken out to meet a target budget or timeframe. Resolve up front that you will be prepared to stop or cancel negotiations if an impasse is reached. In other words, make sure you know when to walk away, which if you do will potentially exert pressure on the party to agree to your terms. It is critical that you listen more than talk, avoiding arguments just to win your point of view. Finally, begin with the end in mind and recognize that you may be setting the stage for potential future negotiations.

3. Negotiate Professionally and Respectfully

Remember to listen more than talk when possible and avoid getting defensive when the other side objects. Use the technique of asking for clarification of a position or specifics when generalizations are used. Recognize the importance of building trust, which comes through your actions and words. Avoid being overly aggressive or arrogant since this approach should increase your odds of success if the other party likes you. Use humor to break any tension during the discussions.

4. Negotiating Techniques

The following are some tactics/reactions that may be helpful in closing a deal:

handling objections: You can simply ignore them or find a way to reduce their importance or counter them with other facts.

remain silent: Often a moment of awkward silence will prompt the other party to talk.

questioning: Use questions to attempt to discover the other party's position.

feigned importance: Ask for or even demand something that is not really that important to you so that you can concede it during discussions. In your preparation, it is advisable to consider some of these.

push for an offer or counteroffer: This potentially forces the other party to lay something on the table.

acknowledge a win: Make the other party feel that they have won on some point.

replace negotiators: This may force a new start.

trigger the fear of missing out: If possible, cause the other side to become concerned that the deal is at risk.

create a sense of urgency: Giving an ultimatum or time requirement can trigger action.

increase your demands: After a concession, seek ever increasing demands.

discuss several offers, one better than another: This may force the hand of the other party.

raise a question regarding goals: Force the other party to clarify their goals. ("Is this that important to you or is it this other point?")

introduce new objections: Create concerns by introducing last-minute obstacles.

final end push: Request a small concession at the very end before you finalize the deal.

PERSUADING OTHERS

Trust me when I say persuading others is a critically important subject with proven principles impactful to leadership and day-to-day interactions, whether they be your employees, kids, spouse, or potential customers. Once you understand the principles, you will recognize how they are often used on you, overtly and subconsciously, by successful salespeople.

Persuasion: The art and science of influencing people's beliefs, attitudes, intentions, or behaviors with a primary purpose of getting others to take actions that are in their own best interest while also benefitting you. It is about moving others from point A to point B, a place where they will act. Note that my definition mentions "science," which refers to several natural human instincts that can be tapped into. These instincts were captured as "influence principles" first highlighted in a 1984 publication by Dr. Robert Cialdini, *Influence: The Psychology of Persuasion* and with a recent book in 2016, *Pre-Suasion: A Revolutionary Way to Influence and Persuade*. Cialdini suggests that there are seven influence principles that are the science behind how humans are wired, and each of us responds positively to the principles, like it or not.

Using these principles is contextual, meaning you need to know what you are trying to accomplish in a specific situation. It is also important to understand that persuading others to comply with a certain behavior is not about manipulation or deceit; it is about understanding human behavior and using the principles to achieve an outcome beneficial to everyone.

Examples are included in the following to further explain how the principles may be applied in day-to-day interactions:

> **reciprocity**: Offering something that someone may feel obliged to repay. This requires reminding someone of how you have helped them previously. An alternative approach is to ask someone for a favor, which, as the saying goes, creates a friend for life.

> **commitment or consistency**: Doing what we say we will. Get someone or a team to commit to something, making them part of the solution, which engenders further commitment. This may be as simple as getting agreement on a charter for a specific project. Consider it a "foot in the door" approach.

social proof: Feeling validated by following what others do. If others are doing something, then so should we. To accomplish this, it is helpful to gain the buy-in of key peer leaders, those who others may look up to.

authority: Feeling a sense of obligation and duty to those who hold positions of authority or who are experts in their fields. You need to demonstrate to others that you have relevant knowledge and expertise and position in the organization.

liking: Feeling or creating a sense of likability. We like those who are like us and thus are generally influenced by them—a trust factor of sorts. This is an earned leadership type trait, earned by providing honest feedback, genuine praise, and effective listening. It is about building trust and being authentic. (Refer to chapter 2 Leadership—Management Basics.)

scarcity: Tapping into concerns that you will miss out on something or want something you cannot have, such as "for a limited time only" or "only x left." In a business setting, this is more about creating a sense of urgency—demonstrating the need for change within a certain time.

unity: Positioning someone on your side. This is about creating a shared sense of identity, such as what groups we belong to, what we are trying to achieve, whom we know, etc., in effect leveraging our tribal instincts. To create a shared sense of identity, you need to take time to understand backgrounds, interests, or challenges, tying some to yours, in effect creating the feeling that we are all in this together and are similar.

Everyone can be persuaded, given the right timing and context, although it may take some time. A basic building block of persuasion is context, which creates a relative standard of what's acceptable. The other building block is timing, which dictates what the listener wants. In that we as humans are generally most interested in ourselves, effective persuasion is learning how to consistently talk to people about them, using the most human of skills: empathy; if you do that and apply some of Cialdini's principles, you will increase your chances of successful persuasion.

Supplementing Cialdini's principles is research on change management within an organization: *To Get People to Embrace Change, Emphasize What Will Stay the Same* by M. Venus, D. Stam, and D. van Knippenberg in the August 15, 2018, Harvard Business Review. Their research suggests that while it is important for leaders to explain how an envisioned change will result in a better and more appealing future, to overcome resistance and build support requires that leaders communicate an appealing vision of change *in combination with* a vision of continuity, i.e., what will stay the same and "what makes us in the organization who we are."

Aristotle, who pioneered the art of persuasion, identified the most important element as *pathos* or the persuader's ability to connect with the feelings, desires, wishes, fears, and passions of the audience. Per Aristotle in *Rhetoric*, an ancient Greek treatise, "Persuasion may come through the hearers when the speech stirs their emotions. Our judgments when we are pleased and friendly are not the same as when we are pained and hostile."

5 PERSONAL TOOLS

In addition to having a knowledge of process tools, you should be proficient in certain "personal tools," which will enable you to stand out while improving your employability and/or advancement opportunities. The ability to effectively manage your time is just one of those.

Time Management

There are only twenty-four hours in a day and what you do during them can be within your control to a large extent. Shown below are time management tips, helpful even if you can only implement a few of them. Effectively managing your time is simpler than you may think. It does however require focus and discipline, adherence to some basic guidelines, and use of a task prioritization tool, such as the quadrant prioritization matrix, popularized by Steven Covey, a productivity expert.

Time management is a life skill that you can and should learn. Using best practices can change your life. Working smarter, not harder can be accomplished! Follow these guidelines:

1. Assess your current state to find out where you may be wasting time.
2. Set time limits for tasks.
3. Make use of any wait or downtime.
4. Learn to delegate to others.
5. Establish routines when possible (e.g., respond to emails during a specific time period).
6. Set time limits for completing tasks, which forces you to focus and be more efficient.
7. Learn to say no, declining opportunities.
8. Focus on one task at a time when possible.

9. Take frequent breaks, keeping your mental and physical states at peak levels. Studies suggest working for fifty-two minutes and then taking a seventeen-minute break.
10. Use a time management/prioritization system that enables you to separate activities into quadrants based on their urgency and importance. Update the matrix each evening.

What follows is a tool, a prioritization matrix, that you can copy and begin to employ for daily activities.

Definitions associated with this matrix:

- *urgent*: requires immediate attention
- *importance*: a measure of the impact on you and/or your organization/team

As the matrix indicates, your focus should be on the urgent task with high importance. Print copies of this tool and use it routinely to assist in your prioritization efforts.

FIRST IMPRESSIONS

This section deals with making a good first impression. I am confident you have heard that people make a judgment regarding a person in the first two seconds of meeting. Knowing what factors are involved in making that impression will give you an advantage. Fortunately, Vanessa Van Edwards researched this subject and published a book: *CAPTIVATE: The Science of Succeeding with People.* I highly recommend it and have summarized the key skills she identified.

- Skill 1: Put your hands up!

Based on an analysis of hand gestures used by the most popular TED talkers, Vanessa found that those who used the most hand gestures were the most popular. This fact was confirmed in a study of hiring of job candidates conducted by Gifford, Ng, and Wilkinson over thirty years ago. When meeting someone, keep your hands visible, not in your pockets.

- Skill 2: Stand like a winner.

Projecting an air of confidence is essential as it will make you appear to be a winner. Vanessa advises that to display a winner's posture, you should keep your shoulders down and back, aim your chin, chest, and forehead straight in front of you or slightly up, keep space between your arms and torso—though not too much—and again, keep your hands out of your pockets.

- Skill 3: Look people in the eye.

The right amount of eye contact is a nonverbal sign of goodwill because when you like someone, you look at him or her more.

- Skill 4: Use nontypical conversation starters.

A study revealed the following order of conversation starters from most to least interesting:

- o   What was the highlight of your day?

o   What personal passion project are you working on?

o   Has anything exciting come up in your life?

o   What's your story?

o   What brings you here?

o   What do you do?

o   How are you?

Try using these questions and skills in your next encounter. You will make a positive impression.

ETIQUETTE

While most organizations have relaxed their dress codes and moved to a more laid-back culture, there is still a need to understand and adhere to basic etiquette, which is generally never taught. The following highlights important rules applicable in both business and personal settings. Since they are US-oriented guidelines, it is important to research expectations in countries you may be traveling to.

1. **Handshake (may be less relevant now since COVID)**

A handshake is critical in making an impression, good or bad. It exhibits your confidence, friendliness, and pleasing personality:

- You should be firm but not overpowering. A limp handshake gives the impression of weakness.
- A handshake should last between two and five seconds. Anything shorter can suggest you are in a hurry.
- Make eye contact during a handshake and offer a sincere smile.
- Shake hands in an up-and-down motion, generally no more than three times.
- The greeting during a handshake should include his or her name and a pleasantry such as "nice to meet you, Ms. James."

2. **Dining**

How you handle yourself during a meal is another opportunity to make an impression. A big challenge I always have is: Which plate is my bread plate? Answer: It is always the one to the left of your water glass. Here are some tips to hone your aptitude for general dining etiquette:

- Arrive on time.
- Turn off your phone.
- Shake hands and/or speak to everyone, maintaining eye contact while concentrating on remembering people's names by repeating them during the introduction.
- Ideally, wait to sit until your host sits.

- Place your napkin on your lap immediately. If you leave during the meal, place your napkin on your chair so the waitstaff know you plan to return.
- If someone else is paying for the meal, do not order the most expensive item.
- When ordering a drink, follow the lead of your host. Generally, it is best not to order an alcoholic beverage at a business meal.
- Check out the place setting. (See photo that follows.) Utensils are generally placed in the order of their use. And yes, the bread plate is always to the left of your plate.

Image Credit: the kitchn

- Handling bread: If you are the first person to take bread from a basket, offer the basket (holding it) to the person on your left and then pass it around the table to the right.
- Handling butter: It is polite to only get butter once from the butter dish. Use the butter knife and place a dollop on the side of your bread plate.

- Eating bread: Tear a piece of bread and butter each piece as you eat it, instead of buttering the entire piece of bread and then tearing off pieces.
- Don't start eating until everyone at the table has been served.
- Eating soup: The proper way to eat soup is to dip the spoon sideways at the edge of the bowl closest to you and then skim from the front of the bowl to the back. Drink the soup from the edge of the spoon, instead of putting the whole spoon into your mouth.
- Don't blow on hot food to cool it down. Stirring will actually cool soup faster.
- Cut your meat one piece at a time instead of cutting it into several bite-size pieces. For salads however, it is best to cut the lettuce into bite-size pieces.
- Don't talk with your mouth open.
- Don't place your elbows on the table.
- Never blow your nose into a napkin.
- To signal that you are done, place your fork, with tines facing up, and knife side-by-side on your plate in the four o'clock position.
- A classy move is to resist efforts by the wait staff to remove your finished plate until everyone else is finished. Otherwise, you are potentially signaling to a slow eater that he or she needs to hurry up.

3. **Introductions**

Make introductions simple by remembering this rule: *speak to the person you wish to honor first.* For instance, "Grandma, meet my friend Jason"/a guest of honor, then someone attending an event/a client and then anyone in the company, including the CEO.

4. **General**

- Give cues that you are paying attention by nodding when someone else is speaking. Avoid interrupting them.
- Be polite and professional in every form of communication.
- Avoid email wars (i.e., raising issues that are best handled person-to-person).
- Keep your workspace clean and neat.

- Show respect for shared areas, cleaning up after yourself, replenishing paper in the copy machine, etc.
- Avoid discussion of politics, sex, or religion and watch your language.
- Minimize complaining or whining.
- Always say please and thank you.
- Turn off your phone during meetings.

While there are several other guidelines, mastering most of these critical ones will demonstrate a level of professionalism not exhibited by many.

6 CHANGING BEHAVIOR

"Knowledge is not power; it is potential. *Action is power.* And inspiration is the spark that puts knowledge into action."

—C. D. James

As the quote suggests, "action is power," and personal action and change are required to make the improvements identified in this book. Change management or habit formation may be the most important skill if you are truly intent on personal success.

It has been reported that it takes anywhere from two to eight months to change a behavior. Regardless of the time it takes, how does one form a new habit? I have identified the following steps and/or guiding principles:

- Focus on one change at a time.
- Commit to work on changing your behavior for eight weeks.
- Set seemingly oversimplistic goals that will help turn a habit into automatic behavior over time.
- If possible, share your change plan with someone else since that will help create accountability.
- Expect that there will be roadblocks along the way. Don't let them bother you if they occur.
- To eliminate a troublesome habit or behavior, decide the behavior change to replace it.
- Celebrate your accomplishments (i.e., set up a personal reward for successful completion of each goal).

Try these for at least eight weeks, one change/habit at a time. You will be amazed at the results.

7 TECHNOLOGY TOOLS

As mentioned in the introduction, we are in the midst of the fourth Industrial Revolution, characterized by technological innovations such as artificial intelligence, bots, drones, big data, virtual reality, blockchains, self-driving vehicles, etc. There is an explosion of software technologies that are remaking the way we work and interact with each other. A scary projection is that these changes could impact up to 50 percent of existing jobs. In this regard, employers expect employees to be proficient in a growing number of technology tools, from software that assists in data analysis to that which enables online collaboration, especially as COVID has driven the popularity of working from home. To ensure your ongoing—and in fact, lifetime—employability, it is important to be able to use many of the tools included in this chapter.

The Basics

It should go without saying that the ability to use the Microsoft suite of products is essential: Word, Excel, and PowerPoint. Increasingly, there is a need to know and be able to use the advanced features of each software such as:

- pivot tables in Excel
- animations or videos to illustrate a point in PowerPoint
- links between sections of a Word document

Artificial Intelligence / Generative AI

This is a relatively new technology that has the potential to revolutionize a wide range of industries. Hence, it is potentially very important to your employability to understand it. What is it? Generative AI is a type of artificial intelligence that is designed to create new content, such as images, music, text, or video, based on a given input. It uses deep-learning models and neural networks to analyze patterns in large datasets and generates new content that resembles the original data.

One of the main benefits of generative AI is that it can automate the creative process, allowing businesses and individuals to generate large amounts of original content quickly and efficiently. For example, generative AI can be used to create personalized product recommendations, design custom logos, or generate realistic 3D models for virtual reality environments.

Another potential impact of generative AI is its ability to enhance human creativity and problem-solving skills. By using generative AI as a tool to assist in the creative process, humans can explore new ideas and generate more innovative solutions to complex problems. Microsoft has introduced a service call Copilot, which includes AI models (OpenAI GPT-4) and has been implemented across its suite of applications. Reportedly, this application will be able to generate text automatically based on information included in other documents.

While ChatGPT has emerged as one of the more popular AI-related tools, others include Stable Diffusion and Midjourney for creating images. Bing, Microsoft's search engine, offers several AI-powered products, including:

- *intelligent answers*: Bing uses natural language processing and machine learning algorithms to provide intelligent answers to user queries. These answers are displayed at the top of the search results page and provide users with a quick and concise answers.
- *visual search*: Bing's visual search allows users to search for information using images instead of text. Users can upload an image or take a picture with their phone's camera and Bing will provide information about the object in the image, such as its name, description, and where to buy it.
- *personalized recommendations*: Bing uses machine learning algorithms to personalize search results for each user based on their search history, location, and other factors. This helps users find relevant content more quickly and easily.
- *Bing Ads*: Bing's advertising platform uses machine learning to optimize ad targeting and bidding. Advertisers can use Bing Ads

to reach a specific audience based on factors such as age, gender, location, and search history.

AI is rapidly growing, and I recommend that a good way to learn the high-level principles is to take a course through Coursera—"AI for Everyone."

online meeting/communication tools: Whether it is for setting up meetings for business or connecting with family, there are several applications available, and you should learn how to use them, beyond just a rudimentary understanding. Popular applications today include Zoom, Google Meet, Microsoft Teams, and Salesforce's Slack.

project management: There are many software options, some more appropriate for the methodology being used and the complexity of the project. An experienced project manager will be able to suggest appropriate software. Here are some popular project management software and the pros and cons of each:

1. **Trello**: Trello is a visual project management tool that uses boards, lists, and cards to help teams organize and prioritize their work. The tool is simple to use and has a free version for personal projects. Some pros of Trello are its user friendly interface, real-time updates, and integration with other tools, such as Slack and Google Drive. However, some cons of Trello include limited functionality for complex projects, a lack of advanced reporting, and limited customization options.

2. **Asana**: Asana allows teams to track their work, organize tasks, and collaborate in real time. Some pros of Asana include its flexible project management features, easy-to-use interface, and integration with other tools, such as Slack and Google Drive. However, some cons of Asana include a relatively steep learning curve for new users, limited customization options, and a higher cost compared to other project management tools.

3. **Monday.com**: Monday.com offers a visual and intuitive interface that can be customized to fit the needs of any team. Some pros of Monday.com include its flexibility, real-time updates, and integration with other tools, such as Slack and Google Drive.

However, some cons of Monday.com include a higher cost compared to other project management tools, limited functionality for complex projects, and a lack of advanced reporting.

4. **Basecamp**: Basecamp focuses on collaboration and communication among team members. Some pros of Basecamp include its easy-to-use interface, real-time updates, and integration with other tools, such as Slack and Google Drive. However, some cons of Basecamp include limited functionality for complex projects, a lack of customization options, and a higher cost compared to other project management tools.

5. **Jira**: Jira is popular among software-development teams. It allows teams to track and manage tasks, bugs, and issues on a single platform. Some pros of Jira include its powerful project management features, extensive customization options, and integration with other tools, such as GitHub and Bitbucket. However, some cons of Jira include a steep learning curve for new users, a complex interface, and a higher cost compared to other project management tools.

In summary, there are numerous software options available, and each has its own set of advantages and disadvantages. When choosing a project management tool, it is important to consider the needs of your team, the complexity of your projects, and your budget.

In summary, there is numerous project-management software available in the market, and each has its own set of advantages and disadvantages. When choosing a project-management tool, it is important to consider the needs of your team, the complexity of your projects, and your budget.

online design (for presentations): Check out Canva, which is helpful in creating graphics.

data analysis and manipulation: Organizations generate an increasing amount of data, and there is a need to make sense of it. Useful software solutions include Microsoft's Power BI and Salesforce's Tableau. LinkedIn offers a course entitled "Power BI Essential Training."

REFERENCES

Agile Alliance. 2001. "Manifesto for Agile Software Development." Retrieved from https://agilemanifesto.org/.

Bennis, W. G. 2009. *On Becoming a Leader.* Basic.

Buckingham, M., and Coffman, C. 1999. *First, Break All the Rules: What the World's Greatest Managers Do Differently.* Simon & Schuster.

Cialdini, R. B. 2006. *Influence: The Psychology of Persuasion.* HarperCollins.

Cialdini, R. B. 2016. *Pre-Suasion: A Revolutionary Way to Influence and Persuade.* Simon & Schuster.

Collins, J. 2001. *Good to Great: Why Some Companies Make the Leap and Others Don't.* HarperCollins.

Covey, S. R. 2004. *The 7 Habits of Highly Effective People: Powerful Lessons in Personal Change.* Free Press.

Department of the Army. 2012. *Army Leadership Field Manual FM 6-22.* United States Government Printing Office.

Fisher, R., Ury, W. L., and Patton, B. 2011. *Getting to Yes: Negotiating Agreement without Giving In.* Penguin.

Goleman, D. 1995. *Emotional Intelligence: Why It Can Matter More Than IQ.* Bantam.

Heath, C., and Heath, D. 2010. *To Get People to Embrace Change, Emphasize What Will Stay the Same.* Harvard Business Review Press.

Kaplan, R. S., and Norton, D. P. 1996. *The Balanced Scorecard: Translating Strategy into Action*. Harvard Business Review Press.

Lewis, M. 2004. *Moneyball: The Art of Winning an Unfair Game*. W. W. Norton & Company.

Van Edwards, V. 2017. *Captivate: The Science of Succeeding with People*. Penguin.

Printed in the United States
by Baker & Taylor Publisher Services